ROADS Publishing
Taylor's Lane
Dublin 8
Ireland
www.roads.co

First published 2017

2

Don't be a Tourist in Paris: The Messy Nessy Chic Guide

Text and image copyright
© Vanessa Grall
Design and layout copyright
© ROADS Publishing

Art direction by
Alessio Avventuroso

Designed by
Agenzia del Contemporaneo

Printed manufactured and managed by Jellyfish Solutions

British Library Cataloguing in Publication Data.

A catalogue record for this book is available from the British Library.

978-1-909399-97-6

DON'T BE A TOURIST IN PARIS

THE MESSY NESSY CHIC GUIDE

THIS BOOK BELONGS TO

_____

PLEASE RETURN WITH CARE*

QUESTIONABLY LEGITIMATE LIBRARY CARD NO. _____

LOOKS COOL ANYWAY

PARISPHILE BOOKMARKS	PAGE NO.
FOUND A TREASURE ON A VISIT TO...	
ATE LIKE A KING AT...	
GUILTY PLEASURE ALERT:	
THAT PECULIAR PLACE:	
GOOD TIMES AT...	

*IF LOST OR OVERDUE, PLEASE KINDLY CONTACT _____

DON'T BE A TOURIST IN PARIS

THE MESSY NESSY CHIC GUIDE

ROADS

PUBLISHING

Hello there. I don't think we've met properly, not like this anyway. I'm Nessy. Thanks for picking me up off the bookshelf. I know there are a lot of books and guidebooks and bestselling books about Paris, but I thought this city needed something in between. I'm almost certain you and I have one thing in common. We are not tourists. We don't hop on bus tours, never head straight for the major landmarks or settle for the same experience as everyone else. We are insatiably curious. We're even a little too nosey at times, but we are not tourists and this is not a guidebook. Think of me more as your new companion, your closest Parisian confidante, your endless bottle of wine while in Paris. These pages are yours now. Dog-ear them, circle stuff and doodle something wherever I take a pause on the page. This is your living Parisian scrapbook, a place to fill with memories, moments and mishaps as we wander the streets of this enchanting city together.

Perhaps you have already found me on the internet – that little corner of the worldwide web where I planted my flag a few years ago and called it *Messy Nessy Chic*. I write about the unusual, the unknown and the unsung from my room with a view here in Paris, or sometimes from the café downstairs. Over the years, I've received hundreds of emails and behind each and every one of those electronic letters is a story of a character coming to Paris feeling a certain way, hoping to feel a different way.

When it came time, it seemed to me like this was the only way I could write a book about Paris – not laid out by arrondissement, or by the hours of the day, or categorised by a type of activity. This book had to be written around a person's mood; around the cards that life has dealt when you wake up on any given day. And as we know, moods can change from one day to the next, shifting our tastes, style and interests, like a moveable feast: like Paris.

Each chapter of this book is inspired by an email I've received from a reader. Try on every character for size, and every one of them will lead you down a unique Parisian rabbit hole. This book is for all those unanswered emails...

Nessy

What's in this Book

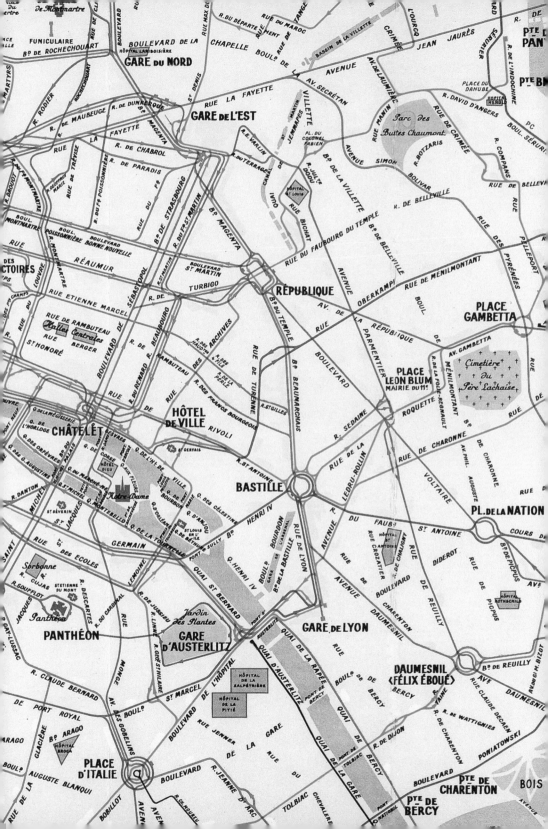

Before You Start

Paris is made up of twenty arrondissements, or districts, that are laid out like a clockwise snail's shell starting from the centre of the city. At the end of every address in this book, you'll find a number between 1 and 20 followed by '*ème*' or '*er*'. That's just how French say '1st, 2nd, 3rd,' etc. You'll get the hang of it.

Don't make exhaustive itineraries for yourself and plan every minute of the day using this book. Think of each address as a clue, pointing you in the direction of an area that's worth getting to know and exploring further. Once you're there, you can always use the handy 'What's Near Me?' index.

The vintage map of Paris that I found in a flea market and used for this book is lovely to look at while finding your bearings, but it's not going to cut it for pinpointing specific locations in the hidden backstreets of the city. You have a smartphone, right? GPS for Google and Apple Maps doesn't use data, so you can find your way around even when you're not connected to Wi-Fi. If you prefer to keep your phone out of sight, you can pick up a map from any tourist office and from most hotels, but for heaven's sake be discreet with it! Remember, we're not tourists.

Paris changes constantly and without warning. Calling the telephone numbers beforehand or checking the websites provided in this book is usually a good idea – especially in August, when half the city goes on holiday and the usual business hours don't apply.

01

The Paris Runaways

Dear Nessy,

I recently came up with this sort of romantic dream to throw caution to the wind and escape to Paris, and now I'm here. The problem is, I'm a little lost, not just in this city but in life. I'm desperate to do anything creative. I tell myself I'm saving up for art supplies, maybe I'll do a short story course. Oh yes, and I'm supposed to be learning French too, not just dreaming. I guess you could say I've come to Paris for some answers. From one Paris runaway to another, where should I start?

Your equally messy,
Fran

This might sound strange, but I didn't actually want to move to Paris. I didn't know anyone here, I had no job prospects and I was absolutely certain that I could never date a French guy. But I, too, was lost. I needed an escape, and so I packed up my South London flat and nervously clutching my French passport with a one-way ticket on the Eurostar, headed for the land of my ancestors and cheese. It wasn't until I picked up a copy of Ernest Hemingway's *A Moveable Feast* that I began to understand how this city could help me. Paris became my muse, my mentor, a source of nostalgia for eras I had never lived through. If there's even the smallest part of you that's drawn to the bohemian way, figure out how to live in Paris at least once in your life. And go with Hemingway's words:

'We ate well and cheaply and drank well and cheaply and slept well and warm together and loved each other.'

Wanderers Welcome: Bohemian Paris

You did it, you made it to Paris and left all that unnecessary baggage behind –
except maybe for the giant suitcase sitting on the bed of your hotel room, which
we'll just have to call home for a few nights until you come up with a better plan.

Okay, time for a drink, but not just anywhere – somewhere you can ponder
the heroes that came here before you; a moody little Parisian joint where you
can step back in time and maybe find F. Scott Fitzgerald quarrelling with Zelda
at the bar.

Dive into Paris

When I'm in a Jim Morrison kind of mood, I find my way to **Le Fanfaron**, a
bar that got me solidly hooked on Paris years ago. Buried in the back alleys of
Bastille, candles drip all over Mexican religious folk art and the walls are like
a museum of vintage concert posters. The slightly mad owner and bartender
Xavier is known for playing out his lovers' tiffs at the bar, knocking back tequila
shots with his eccentric regulars and playing Jimi Hendrix records all night if he
wants to. Order a 'Destroyeur' or try the melon beer and generally have a pretty
rock 'n' roll time. I hope you can still find me drinking here in twenty years' time.
You can check out, but you can never leave.
(*6 rue de la Main d'Or, 11ème; +331 4923 4114 facebook.com/LeFanfaronBar*)

Le Fanfaron

You'll find a warm and cosy welcome at **Le Venus Noir**, the Latin Quarter's hidden bar in a narrow, ancient street. The vaulted cellar carved out of limestone dates back to 1290, and before the French banned absinthe (known then as *la fée verte*; 'the green fairy'), famous poets such as Charles Baudelaire and Arthur Rimbaud were regulars here. The friendly barmen are full of stories if you ask for one, and the walls tell so much history of their own. Oh, and keep in mind that Wednesday night is jam night.
(*25 rue de l'Hirondelle, 6ème; lavenusnoire.net; open from 6pm Mon-Sat and 3pm-9pm on Sundays*)

Le Bar Dix is one of the last true down-and-out dives left in Saint-Germain. Opened in 1955 by a bohemian Spaniard called Mariano, it hasn't had a new lick of paint since the '60s, and don't bother asking for something that isn't sangria, which – be careful – gets stronger as the night goes on. Put a euro in the jukebox and play my favourite French record, 'Le temps de l'amour' by Françoise Hardy. The next song is yours.
(*10 rue de l'Odéon, 6ème; lebar10.com; open every day 5pm-2am*)

First Parisian Dinner Party...

What do Yoko Ono, Chloë Sevigny, Allen Ginsberg and Germaine Greer all have in common? They've all been guests at **Jim Haynes' Parisian dinner parties**. Since the '70s this loveable man has been throwing dinner parties every Sunday for complete strangers in his old artist's studio. The Louisiana-born ex-pat has been called the 'godfather of social networking', following his 1980s series of self-published guides, which listed addresses of local people willing to help or host travellers. Back in 1960s London, he founded the Arts Lab, where John Lennon and Yoko Ono exhibited their first joint artwork, and in 1969, he co-founded *Suck*, an Amsterdam-based magazine celebrating sexual freedom. Basically, he's a pretty cool, free-thinking dude. His dinner parties move into the garden during summer and usually attract up to sixty or seventy guests; travellers, locals, artists, students – anyone is welcome. Sometimes Jim cooks, sometimes his neighbour does, sometimes an invited chef takes over the stove. Guests are just asked to make a contribution and he always breaks even. Don't be shy, Jim likes people who reach out, and he'll introduce everyone to everyone. To attend one of Jim's parties, give him a call or reserve on his website and let him know how many of you there will be.
(*83 rue de la Tombe Issoire, 14ème; +33 1 43 27 17 67; jim-haynes.com*)

Traveller Pit Stops

A place to rest your binoculars and backpacks, **L'Improbable** is a whimsical hideaway inside the shell of an old Parisian garage. Think Wes Anderson's film *Moonrise Kingdom* manifested into a café. This campers' clubhouse serves up

fresh juices, warming soups and healthy sandwiches from a vintage trailer surrounded by old maps, adventure storybooks and bric-a-brac.
(*3-5 rue des Guillemites, 4ème; facebook.com/LimprobableCafe; open Tuesday to Sunday, 12pm-9pm*)

At **Folks & Sparrows** you'll always get a friendly hello from Franck, who spent ten years waiting tables in Brooklyn before he returned to Paris to open his own joint. A bit of a tumbleweed himself, he likes to exchange travel stories while he makes you a great cup of coffee or the most Instagrammable baguette sandwich in his rustic café, with folk music as a soundtrack. Seek it out after a good stomp around the Haut Marais neighbourhood nearby.
(*14 rue Saint-Sébastien, 11ème; +33 9 81 45 90 99*)

L'Improbable Café

Café Loustic is what I like to call a 'Franglais' coffee spot. Both an international and a local crowd seek out this Parisian nook for flawless lattes and the living-room style ambience, adorned with cosy kilim sofas and vintage Hermès wallpaper. Kick back and relax with a lazy day's worth of magazines and trouble-free Wi-Fi.
(*40 rue Chapon, 3ème; cafeloustic.com; open every day for breakfast until 6pm*)

Le Square Gardette is an old sewing shop turned eclectic neighbourhood hang-out, open from morning to night. Eat well, stick around, and cosy up with the resident cat who lounges where he pleases, on the bookshelves or stretching out across the sofas. Get a feel for the local neighbourhood on the nearby *rue Saint-Maur*.
(*24 rue Saint-Ambroise, 11ème; squaregardette.fr; open every day*)

A Clubhouse to Call Home (and plug in your laptop)

We all had some kind of clubhouse as kids, didn't we? Whether it was a treehouse, a backyard den, a bedroom duvet fort, or a secret meeting place in an old shack by the railway tracks, we all needed a little hideout to call our own. For me, that never really changed and I think every aspiring entrepreneur, freelancer, dreamer, risk-taker or runaway needs a clubhouse here in Paris – no passwords or secret handshakes necessary.

Rev Your Entrepreneurial Engines Here

You could mistake **Le Comptoir Générale** for a forgotten, once grand African hotel, a social club in Senegal or a Stanley Kubrick film set. Filled with eclectic furniture and elaborate props to take you to a faraway place and time, this theatrical wonderland hidden behind the trendy Canal Saint-Martin is host to film nights, art exhibitions, vintage sales, environmental conferences, foodie pop-ups – you name it. On weekdays, the venue associates itself with young social entrepreneurs embarking on eco-social-cultural adventures. Come the weekend, DJ's and live bands take over the hall and Sundays are for festive family brunching.

(80 Quai de Jemmapes, 10ème; lecomptoirgeneral.com; open every day, 11am–2pm)

Change the World with Nutella

When planning world domination, or, you know, just writing a new blog post, I need a good quiet nook to curl up in with my laptop like a cat, flashing my most embarrassing socks. The environment needs to be inspiring and the Wi-Fi reliable. Seek out **Nuage Café**, as in Cloud Café, as in, yes, this is what it's like to work on Cloud 9. For €4 an hour or €16 a day, you can set yourself up in a beautiful two-storey workspace, take meetings, order unlimited artisanal coffee (made with a real-deal coffee machine), raid the snack buffet all day long (Nutella and cookies included), borrow iPads, use free lockers, and generally make yourself at home.

There's a great history behind this celestial workplace too. Originally part of an old church built in the fourteenth century and later a university, it was within these very walls that a libertine writer by the name of Savinien de Cyrano de Bergerac studied during the 1600s, and it would become the inspiration for the famous French drama *Cyrano de Bergerac*. You're also next to *place Maubert*, where one of the first universities in the world, l'Université de Paris (today known as La Sorbonne), was founded right out in the open square, where students and intellectuals gathered to listen to the first professors of Europe. Students would mostly be taught in Latin, and the classical language was so often heard spoken around the neighbourhood that it eventually took on its name as the '*Quartier Latin*'. By the thirteenth century, the Latin Quarter was the intellectual centre of the world. So not a bad place to start, right?

(*14 rue des Carmes, 5ème; nuagecafe.fr*)

Opposite: Le Comptoir Générale
Left: Nuage Café

Home Sweet Playhouse

Covered in beautiful street art murals, the canal-side **Pavillon des Canaux** is set up like a cosy countryside home, complete with a kitchen, bedrooms, living rooms, bathrooms, and plenty of nooks and crannies, any of which you're welcome to claim as your hang-out spot. If you want to call a meeting with your gang at one of the long tables, do it. If you want to get in the bathtub and write an email, do it. Tempting distractions range from tournaments of *pétanques* (boules) on the sunny terrace to brownie bake-offs in the 1950s kitchen. (*39 quai de la Loire, 19ème; pavillondescanaux.com/en*).

By the Railway Tracks

If you make a trip to the legendary Paris flea markets (pg. 49), drop in at **La Recyclerie**, a converted old train station on the abandoned tracks of the 'Little Belt' railroad, a surviving relic of a bygone era, closed since 1934 (pg. 165). There's always something going on here, whether it's a DIY workshop, vintage sale, small yoga classes or foodie events in the urban garden along the old railway tracks. (*83 boulevard Ornano, 18ème; larecyclerie.com; +33 1 42 57 58 49*)

Pavillon des Canaux

Books & Hammocks

Paris seems to have figured out that its disused churches make perfect shelters for entrepreneurial vagabonds. **L'Archipel** is another beautiful nineteenth-century house of worship turned co-working space and 'centre of collective innovation', where you can rent a workspace from €170 a month. Give it a test drive on a Sunday, when their café does a mean brunch. Take a siesta afterwards in one of the hammocks hanging from the alcoves.
(*26 rue de Saint-Pétersbourg, 8ème; larchipel.paris*)

Going for Broke: the City on a Budget

So you're low on funds. Strangely, around the end of every month the same thing happens to me...

Feasts in a Salad Bowl

Chez Gladines is where Parisians go to eat like kings for around €10. Order the gigantic French salads and then come back to try the authentic grandmother specialities. They have five restaurants dotted around Paris but if you have the freedom to choose, the original one in the 13th arrondissement is the most charming.
(*30 rue des cinq Diamants, 13ème; open every day for lunch and dinner; gladines.com*)

Dinner for your Big Group of Equally Broke Friends

Even more cheap and cheerful is **La Cantine de Belleville**. It's amusingly chaotic and a favourite with hungry bohemian Parisian students on a budget. Big portions, bargain prices.
(*108 boulevard de Belleville, 20ème; +33 1 43 15 99 29*)

A Clandestine Lunch beneath Napoleon's Temple

Most Parisians have no idea there's a restaurant hidden inside one of the city's most central monuments. Forget the glitzy truffle and caviar houses of *Place de la Madeleine* and duck into a vaulted eighteenth-century secret lunch spot. **Le Foyer de la Madeleine** can be accessed through a small side door of the Romanesque temple that dominates the square behind the flower market. A favourite with in-the-know customers working in the area, the service is provided by adorable ladies of the quartier who volunteer for the non-profit underground restaurant. You can get a complete meal for only €10 (€15 if you're not a member), which includes a starter, main course and dessert. The food is delicious, the atmosphere is unique, and the gains are destined to help the less fortunate.
(*Place de la Madeleine, 8ème; foyerdelamadeleine.fr; open Mon- Fri for lunch*)

L'Ave Maria

Inside the Fortune Teller's Parisian Lair
Take a trip to South America through the doors of **L'Ave Maria**, where Ana Maria serves arguably the cheapest beer in Paris and pitchers of frozen margarita for sharing with friends. The kitchen serves generous and delicious plates of world fusion cuisine, although they're not quite as generously priced as the drinks. It doesn't get much more bohemian than this joint.
(*1 rue Jacquard, 11ème; +33 1 47 00 61 73; open until 2am*)

If you have €10 in your Pocket
At **Pizza Popolare**, one of the most hyped up Italian restaurants in town, you can get a wood fired Margherita for €5 or go all out and add potatoes, bacon, eggs and herbs on top for a tenner. They don't take reservations but early birds can avoid a long wait.
(*111 rue Réaumur, 2ème; +33 1 42 21 30 91; open every day for lunch & dinner*)

What would life have been like as a student in 1960s rock 'n' roll Paris? Try the **Café Basile**, next to the Sciences Po university campus in St Germain, and you'll find out. They have a €10 student menu and very good deals at happy hour.
(*34 rue de Grenelle, 7ème; cafe-le-basile.com; open every day*)

Lunch or dinner aboard the floating restaurant **L'Antipode** won't set you back more than a tenner, which will get you a soup to start, an overflowing tostada, plus dessert.
(*55 Quai de la Seine, 19ème; penicheantipode.fr; open every day for lunch and dinner*)

At **Les Fondus de la Raclette**, get stuffed on runny cheese, oven potatoes and charcuterie with the €10 lunch deal in this urban ski chalet.
(*Two locations: 19 rue Joseph Dijon, 18ème and 107 avenue Parmentier, 11ème; lesfondusdelaraclette.com; open every day*)

Three for Free
1   Hidden down a cobblestone street, you can eat for free four nights a week at **Tribal Café**. On Wednesdays and Thursdays, get complimentary mussels and fries when you order any drink, and on Fridays and Saturdays it's the house couscous on offer. This is not grand gastronomy but a perfectly respectable meal. Beers start at €3.80 or €3 during happy hour.
(*3 Cour des Petits Ecuries, 10ème; +33 1 47 70 57 08*)
2   Pack a bottle of vino, a blanket and cosy up under the stars for an open-air movie night in the park at **La Villette**. From late July to the end of August, both French and English language films, modern and classic, are played for free on a giant outdoor screen on the park's lawn.
(*Terrasse du Parc, 19ème; lavilette.com; Wed-Sun*)

3   **National museums** are free to the public on the first Sunday of every month. (*Free events around the city are listed on ParisGratuit.com*)

A Roof over your Head: 5 Affordable Stays

1   **Mije** (*4ème; mije.com/auberge-jeunesse-paris*)
2   **El Dorado Hotel** (*17ème; eldoradohotel.fr*)
3   **Hôtel du Nord le Paris Velo** (*10ème; hoteldunord-leparivelo.com*)
4   **Generator Hostel** (*10ème; generatorhostels.com*)
5   **Les Piaules** (*11ème; espiaules.com*)

Frugal Fashion Fixes

Instead of yard sales, Parisians have what's called a '**Vide Grenier**' or a '**Vide Dressing**', which literally entails emptying their attics and closets. But of course Paris doesn't exactly have much yard space, so neighbours and groups of friends traditionally get together on weekends to organise a big communal street sale on the local boulevard, or sometimes they set up shop in an empty gallery space they've rented for the day. There is treasure to be found. (*Most are listed on Vide-Greniers.org/75-Paris for household goods and Vide-Dressing.org/75-Paris for spring-cleaning closets*)

Go digging at **Kilo Shop** where, quite simply, vintage clothes are priced by weight, with Levi's 501s weighing 700g for €14 and vintage furs weighing 1.5kg for €45. (*Several locations, including 65 rue de la Verrerie, 4ème and 125 Bld St Germain, 6ème; open every day*)

Usually Hiring Ex-Pats

So you can picture yourself working in a cute Parisian café or bar to help fund your dream. Here are a few spots I've noticed are ex-pat friendly for when you're dropping off your résumé around town...

1   **Cosi** (*54 rue de Seine, 6ème; open every day, 12-11pm*)
2   **KB Café Shop** (*53 avenue Trudaine; 9ème; open every day for breakfast until 6.30pm*)
3   **Mary Celeste** (*1 rue Commines, 3ème; open for dinner every day, 6pm-2am*)
4   **La Buvette** (*67 rue Saint-Maur, 11ème; open Wednesday to Sunday*)
5   **Broken Biscuits** (*10 Passage Rochebrune, 11ème; open Wednesday to Sunday*)

Handy Links for Working in Paris

·   The FUSAC website contains classified ads and advertisements to serve the English-speaking communities in Paris: *Fusac.fr*
·   What you need to know about working in France as a foreigner: *Etudiantdeparis. fr/node/18*
·   Pick up an extra restaurant shift: *Extracadabra.com*

Above: Fontaine Moliere
Left: Rue Vivienne

Desperately Seeking Inspiration: Creative Havens

The good news is, if you're trying to overcome a creative block, facing a scary life decision or generally lacking inspiration, you're in the right city. Aimlessly wandering the Parisian streets to let your mind breathe is half a plan, but let's steer you around a few corners where you might find a light at the end of the tunnel.

Writer's Retreat

Hoping to find that inspiring spot to produce your best work yet? Start with an early morning at the café of the **Petit Palais**. Not so 'petit', rather both spectacular and serene, the covered marble terrace of the café overlooking the inner courtyard is writer's magic.
(*Avenue Winston Churchill, 8ème; petitpalais.paris.fr; open Tuesday to Sunday, 10am-6pm*)

At the cosy 1930s-themed tea room **La Chambre Aux Oiseaux**, settle into an armchair, order one too many slices of their delicious homemade cakes, and admire the gorgeous wallpaper and the antique knick-knacks all around. The words should start to pour out of you.
(*48 rue Bichat, 10ème Paris; +33 1 40 18 98 49; open every day, 10am-6.30pm, except Monday it closes at 5pm*)

Hidden behind the *boulevard Saint-Germain*, there's a passage that has always been one of my favourite spots to scribble away in a notebook with a glass of wine while watching the world go by. Pick any of the café terraces along the cobblestones of **Cour du Commerce Saint-André**. I like to try a different one every time. As dusk approaches, the passage is lit by colourful string lights; a perfect snapshot of Paris at night.
(*Cour du Commerce Saint-André, 6ème*)

Sometimes I need the background noise of a Parisian café to jolt my writing, and when it's cold and raining outside, it doesn't get more atmospheric than the old **Café Charbon**. This century-old brasserie has kept its weathered zinc bar, art nouveau panels and tarnished mirrors to help you imagine a scene straight out of the Belle Époque. It's a charismatic local spot where you can stick around as long as you like, occasionally ordering *un café* while drafting your memoirs.
(*109 rue Oberkampf, 11ème; +33 1 43 57 55 13; open every day, 9am-2am*)

Artist's Room with a View

Inside the oldest building in Montmartre, where artists like Auguste Renoir once kept a studio, behind an inconspicuous door, you can step into the shoes of a bohemian painter living in turn-of-the-century Paris. At the **Musée de Montmartre**, one of the old artist studios has been restored and reimagined just as Renoir might have left it. Up close and personal in the private world of an artist-in-residence, feel the warmth of summer shining through the atelier windows and smell the paint slowly drying in the sun. Brush your hands over the dusty work table, where once the ghosts of this studio would have sat mixing their colour palettes and painting their muses. Doesn't every bohemian at heart dream of a humble existence in a Parisian studio in Montmartre?

Outside in the gardens, you can see as far as the rolling hills beyond the city limits. Follow the sloping path that goes past the beehives and you'll find yourself with a front-row seat to the **Clos Montmartre**, one of Paris's last working vineyards, which produces 1,500 half-litre bottles each year.
(*12-14 rue Cortot, 18ème; museedemontmartre.fr; open every day, 11am-6pm*)

Musée de Montmartre

Find your Muse

Take a life-drawing workshop at one of the oldest art academies in Paris and you might just find yourself sitting in the very same chair where Picasso, Manet, Delacroix or Cezanne sat sketching their models a century ago. The unchanged atelier of **L'Académie de la Grande Chaumière**, founded in 1904, is open to the public for afternoon sketching workshops, Monday to Saturday, except on Wednesday when there's an evening session from 7-10pm. No reservations are necessary, just show up with paper and pencils, and there is no teacher, just the model. If you're looking for some guidance, lessons are available.

(*14 rue de la Grande Chaumière, 6ème; +33 1 43 26 13 72; student rates start at €13 per class. See the Free Workshop and School sections of the website for all prices and timetables: Grande-chaumiere.fr/en*)

A Secret World of Pastel

'African violet', 'red of Venice', 'Naples yellow', 'Green suede', and 'Purple from Mars' – these are the names of colours created by the oldest pastel manufacturer in the world, **La Maison du Pastel**, which is waiting for you at the back of a hidden courtyard. The workshop, where they've been producing over 1,200 shades of Roché pastels since 1906, is open only one afternoon a week, when you can explore their endless drawers filled with colours waiting to tell a story. The assorted sets would make a meaningful gift for any aspiring artist.

(*20 rue Rambuteau, 3ème; +33 1 40 29 00 67; lamaisondupastel.com; open Thursday, 2pm-6pm, check the website in advance for any unusual hours*)

Sketch-Worthy Scenes

- **The Medici Fountain** (*Jardin de Luxembourg, 6ème*)
- **Musée Bourdelle** (*16-18 rue Antoine Bourdelle, 15ème; bourdelle.paris.fr; open Tuesday to Sunday, 10am-6pm*)
- **La Galerie d'anatomie comparée** (*pg. 74*)
- **Square George Cain** (*rue Payenne, 3ème; open every day, 8am-8.30pm*)

Sketch Me Something Here

Musée Bourdelle

Get your Hands Dirty

In the old studio of Marcel Duchamp (the guy who submitted a urinal to an exhibition and called it art), **Rrose Sélavy Ateliers D'arts** is where Parisians come to draw, paint, sculpt (nude models included), knit, carve, collage – if it's fun and creative, this place does it. Go for a one-off trial class or sign up for a term. Courses are intimate, with no more than twelve students per class. The atelier is also home to a quirky café serving fresh snacks to keep the creativity flowing. (*5 rue Fromentin, 9ème; rroseselavy.net; trial classes start from €32*)

Crafter's Supply Run

Whether it's homemade jewellery or a mixed-media art project on the agenda, at the top of your list should be the Paris flea market *les Puces de Saint-Ouen*. You'll want to track down two spots in particular within the labyrinthine flea market, which is divided up into several smaller markets, each with their own name and character. In the *Marché Dauphine (132-140 rue des Rosiers, 93400 Saint-Ouen; marche-dauphine.com*), you'll find a bead, button and bric-a-brac heaven at **Daniel et Lili**, located at stand 128 on the ground floor, in front of the orange Futuro House (a big 1960s spaceship).

Seek out more treasure in the market across the street known as *Marché des Vernaisons (99 rue des Rosiers, 93400 Saint-Ouen*) and weave your way through the tiny alley streets to a shop called **Tombée du Camion**, which literally translates as 'fallen off the truck'. They specialise in vintage deadstock by the truckload, from spare toy parts and bizarre novelty items to missing pieces from your childhood that you never knew you'd lost.
(*Marché Dauphine is open Friday mornings, Sat & Sun 10am-6pm, Mon 10am-5pm; Marché des Vernaisons is open Sat & Sun 10am-6pm, Mon 10am-5pm*).

Musicians on the Road

In a corner of Paris where the rock 'n' roll set naturally gravitate, **La Maroquinerie** is an old leather factory turned restaurant and concert hall, giving a stage to some of the best emerging indie bands passing through Paris (Coldplay did a gig here before they released their first album in 2000). The restaurant is not to be overlooked and it's definitely worth sticking around after dinner. (*23 rue Boyer, 20ème; lamaroquinerie.fr*)

While you're there, check out **La Bellevilloise** next door; a former workers' union (notice the communist hammer and sickle above the door), it is now a multitasking house of entertainment. It's host to a music club, bar, restaurant and exhibition space, where events range from swing festivals to craft markets. On Sundays it plays host to a jazz brunch (pg. 146). (*19-21 rue Boyer, 20ème; labellevilloise.com*)

Fashion School Dropout

Whether you're a designer, a stylist, or just fancy trying your hand at making your own clothes, at the **Marché St Pierre** in Montmartre you'll be spoilt for choice with unique fabrics and haberdashery to get your creative groove back. (*2 rue Charles Nodier, 18ème; marchesaintpierre.com*)

If you happen to be interested in costume design, the vintage boutique **Casablanca** is famous for reproducing old suits and shirts that they just don't make like they used to. Housed in an old boulangerie behind the *rue Oberkampf* and specialising in clothes and accessories from the 1930s to the 1970s, a lot of the pieces in Casablanca eventually end up on stage at the Opéra Garnier or the Théâtre du Châtelet. (*17 rue Moret, 11ème; casablancapolo.com*)

Chasing Hemingway

If I'm ever asked to hypothetically choose a famous character from the past to have a dinner with, my answer is always going to be Papa Hemingway. It's not just because I'd want to speak endlessly with him about his Paris years, but also for the reason – and surely I can't be alone in thinking this – that Ernest Hemingway is simply the paradigm of what a man strives to be. So yes, I have a big fat crush on Mr Hemingway.

'Lost Generation' Bookshops of the Left Bank

Shakespeare & Company is world renowned for its old-fashioned charm, its Hemingway connection, and that magical feeling you get while ducking and squeezing through the nooks and crannies. There's just one problem; it's usually flooded with tourists. So here's a tip; go at night. It's open until 11pm every

No. 359666

day. Catch an evening reading with Pulitzer prize-winning authors or even a Hollywood actor like Ethan Hawke. Did you know he's a published author? Neither did I, until I wandered in one day to find him doing a book reading. Drop in on a folk band playing in the upstairs library or just take advantage of the golden quiet hour before it closes. Oh, and have you read *The Paris Wife* by Paula McLain? It's written from the perspective of Ernest Hemingway's first wife Hadley during their years in Paris. It's like reading a sequel to *A Moveable Feast*. Both titles are always in stock at Shakespeare & Co.

(*37 rue de la Bûcherie, 5ème; shakespeareandcompany.com; open 10am-11pm; check their Facebook page for evening events*)

Tinier, but equally charming and nostalgic, **The Abbey Bookshop** is your off-the-beaten path daytime alternative. Beautiful books piled haphazardly to the ceiling, warm lighting, jazz playing in the background – you can easily spend an hour getting to know an old treasure that tumbled from the shelf just for you.

(*29 rue de la Parcheminerie, 5ème; +33 1 46 33 16 24; open Mon-Sat until 7pm*)

The San Francisco Book Company fills a certain need for any Anglophile spending a good amount of time in Paris. Tucked away on a quiet street and filled floor to ceiling with used books, this is an unfrequented gem where you get a real American 'hello' when you walk in the door. You feel unhurried and at ease while ferreting out romance, sci-fi, guides, classics, cookbooks and much more. The American owner is very knowledgeable but completely unpretentious and great for engaging in some book banter.

(*17 rue Monsieur le Prince, 6ème; sfparis.com; open every day, usually until 9pm*)

Le Pont Traversé Bookshop

Also worth seeking out is the old butcher's bookshop, **Le Pont Traversé**. Once a former *grande boucherie* of the 1800s, it is now crammed full of rare French books. Cast your eyes over the golden bulls' heads above the windows of the royal blue façade, indicating that this corner shop hasn't always been selling books, and look out for the meat hooks on the ceiling.
(*62 rue de Vaugirard, 6ème; +33 1 45 48 06 48; closed on Sundays*)

What would a romantic stroll along the Seine be without **les bouquinistes**? To get their literary fix, Hemingway and other great artistes browsed the very same book stands that still squat on the banks of the Seine today. The mayor's office makes it a priority that the 250+ Parisian bouquinistes stay solvent. Back in the eighteenth century, however, the bouquinistes would have been regularly chased across bridges and along the Seine by established bookshop owners who were losing business to the illegitimate sellers. Even with eBooks and iPads threatening their existence today, they're still selling dog-eared vintage print from their open-air boxes the same way they did a hundred years ago.
(*My favourites are along the Quai de la Tournelle, 5ème, and the Quai Malaquais, 6ème; open most days/if and when they feel like it*)

Wine Bar in a Bookshop

At an intimate literary café hiding in plain sight in the beating heart of the Marais, you can enjoy an excellent Pouilly-Fuissé while thumbing through books, or mingle with the international intellectual crowd over an evening glass of cognac. **La Belle Hortense** celebrates the marriage of wine and books with locals and newbies alike, playing David Bowie on the stereo and offering charcuterie and sharing plates from the sister restaurant across the street. Over the weekend it can get slightly crowded later in the evenings, but on Monday and Tuesday nights it's just the regulars, who love a friendly chat. Take a book or a bottle away with you and hop over to the other side of the street to see if **Au Petit Fer à Cheval** (pg. 131) has your table ready. Hop back after dessert for another round of booze and books if you like; it's the only wine cave/library in Paris that stays open until two in the morning.
(*31 rue Vieille du Temple, 4ème; +33 1 48 04 71 60; open every day, 5pm-2am*)

Hey! Let's Start a Book Club

If I was to start my own 'Lost Generation' Book Club à la Gertrude Stein, I would make its headquarters at **La Fourmi Ailée**. This cosy teahouse would be the perfect setting, surrounded by the mini library of old books and pretty twinkle lights. Service here is a little slow but this is not the place to grab a quick coffee. In fact, La Fourmi has just about one of the longest tea menus in Paris. Bring a book or bring your own book club.
(*8 rue du Fouarre, 5ème; parisresto.com; open every day, 12pm-12am*)

22 rue Delambre

A Door to the Past

Find an untouched relic of old-world Paris hiding behind the façade of **22 *rue Delambre***, the same street where Hemingway first met Fitzgerald at the Dingo Bar in 1925. If you have the chance to pass by and find 22 *rue Delambre* 'open' (hint: press the intercom button and give a push on weekdays during delivery hours), a real-life time warp awaits. You could also stop in at Hem's more famous old stomping grounds around the corner on the *boulevard Montparnasse*, **La Coupole** and **Le Dome**.
(*6ème; Métro: Vavin*)

A Date with Hem

The secret is out that Mr Hemingway was a regular customer at *Café Flore* and *Les Deux Margots*, rendering them classic tourist stops. Thankfully however, he never mentioned in his books that he was a patron of the time-honored brasserie **La Palette**. Situated in the backstreets of Saint-Germain, spilling out onto the street with its sizeable al fresco tent, a glamorous local crowd gathers after work hours to begin the evening's festivities. Plenty of table-sharing goes on here and plenty of flirtatious tactics – be wary of the house regular in red chinos who likes sending his Jack Russell around to tables of unchaperoned girls to do his groundwork! On summer nights it's buzzing and the champagne is flowing.
(*43 rue de Seine, 6ème; open every day, 8am-2am; +33 1 43 26 68 15*)

After your quintessential Saint-Germain-style apéro, head a few doors down to the appropriately but coincidentally named **Bistro Ernest**. Fall into this charming little neighbourhood gem, which will warm a weary traveller's heart and offer a surprising selection of healthy and vegetarian options for such an authentic French eatery. Having changed hands over the years, but always catering to the local clientele of gallerists who stop in daily to sit at the bar, this spot has been around since Hemingway was.
(*21 rue de Seine Paris, 6ème; Mon-Fri 10am-10pm & Sat 10am-6pm; +33 1 56 24 47 47*)

For an overnight moveable feast, the **Hôtel des Grandes Ecoles** is a hidden oasis on the doorstep of Ernest Hemingway's old apartment at 74 *rue du Cardinal Lemoine*. Cheap and charming rooms.
(*75 rue du Cardinal Lemoine, 5ème; hotel-grandes-ecoles.com*)

Ernest (shall we call him 'Ernie'?) would feel right at home at **Café de l'Industrie**. It's a place that could have been inspired by the author's adventures – part Cuban coffee house, part colonial African gentlemen's club, and part 1920s Parisian bistro.* Let the dim lighting, jazzy ambience and red-wine-fuelled supper be part of your moveable feast.
(*16 rue Saint-Sabin, 11ème; +33 1 47 00 13 53; open every day*)

*Why do they call it a bistro anyway?
Something tells me we're going to be using the word 'bistro' a lot in these pages, so here's a little trivia for you: a Parisian waiter once told me that bistro derives from the Russian word 'bystro'; meaning 'quickly' or 'faster'. During the Russian occupation of Paris in 1815, the Czar's soldiers hounded French waiters with cries of 'Bystro! Bystro!' – so much so that French restaurateurs began calling their establishments 'bistros' to advertise quick service. Fancy that!

Hemingway's Homecoming

On 25 August 1944, Ernest Hemingway was a man on a mission to liberate the Hôtel Ritz from the clutches of Hitler's army. During the World War II Nazi occupation of Paris, the iconic hotel had become the official living quarters of notorious German figures, including Hermann Goering and Joseph Goebbels. As the US army marched towards Paris, Hemingway raced ahead, leading his own private army of resistance fighters. As the story goes, the unlikely band of vigilantes in their commandeered military Jeep dramatically screeched to a halt outside the Ritz, carrying machine guns. Ernest Hemingway had arrived to reclaim his beloved bar, but when met by the concierge, he was informed that the Germans had already left and Mr Hemingway would regrettably not be allowed to enter the hotel carrying a weapon. Checking his gun at the door,

Above: Café de l'Industrie
Opposite: Hemingway Bar at
the Ritz Hotel

the lion-hearted, uniformed writer forged ahead to the old drinking spot of his 'Lost Generation' and allegedly ran up a tab for fifty-one dry martinis. There is also an intriguing albeit unconfirmed story, that in 1956, Hemingway retrieved two trunks from the basement of the hotel that he had secretly stashed there in 1927. His last wife claimed that these trunks held manuscripts from the writer's pre-war reign in Paris, and it was the discovery of these old papers that inspired him to write the memoirs that would become the posthumously published masterpiece *A Moveable Feast*.

So really, if you're as much of a fan of old Papa Hem as I am, how could you not make a pilgrimage to the **Hemingway Bar** at the **Ritz Hotel**? Just the once. Yes, it's expensive, but it's a rite of passage. Arrive early when it opens at 6pm sharp, and sit beside a typewriter and order your dry Martini from the dedicated team of bartenders that would make Hem proud.
(*15 Place Vendôme, 1er; +33 1 43 16 30 30; open every day, 6pm-2am*)

40 Rue Durantin

02

Paris like it is in the Movies
(and on Instagram)

Hi Nessy,

I'm a twenty-six-year-old long-time reader from Australia. Last year, I fell in love with a girl, Christina, from Austria and recently moved all the way from Melbourne to be with her (it's been complicated).

I'm planning a week in Paris with Christina and while I've been lucky enough to visit Paris a number of times before, she has never been. I envy her – Paris for the first time with fresh eyes. The mirror above her desk is covered with photographs of French bakeries and movie stills of Audrey Hepburn in Paris. I'd like to do things we'll both enjoy but I'm also worried that I won't be able to show her the city in a way that will live up to her expectations. I'm a touch overwhelmed and could really use any advice. I just want to give Christina the world. She deserves it, so I'm starting with Paris.

Happy trails to you,
George

Ever heard of the Paris Syndrome? Over twenty years ago, a Japanese psychiatrist working in France identified a peculiar phenomenon affecting tourists visiting the French capital who found themselves overcome with shock from Paris 'not living up to expectations'. Around a million Japanese tourists travel here every year awaiting the fairy-tale vacation they once saw in a movie, and an average of twelve of them leave on a stretcher. My point is, any anxiety you might feel in meeting your or someone else's expectations of Paris is somewhat understandable. The good news is, the real Parisian fairy tale is not lost. Seven years I've been in this city, and not a day goes by that I don't experience some form of wonderment just from standing on a street corner or driving down an undiscovered street on my old putt-putting Mobylette. Stick with me and I'll show you what I mean – I promise it won't involve getting pickpocketed up the Eiffel Tower...

Strolling with Amélie Poulain

I remember watching *Le Fabuleux Destin d'Amélie Poulain* for the first time in my high school French class and once again just before I moved to Paris, but never since. I suppose I was given the impression that the movie had turned Montmartre into a tourist trap of romanticised clichés about Paris and it was a very unfashionable, unappreciated reference to make. In fact, I nearly wrote this chapter without even mentioning her name at all, but to leave Amélie out of these pages would be like forgetting a first love. More than fifteen years on from the film's release, now that the 'Amélie effect' has somewhat died down, her whimsical and playful Paris provides the comforting, impromptu escape from everyday life in the city that we all need sometimes. The film was shot in over eighty city locations, so I won't accompany you to them all; instead I'd like to take you down a single street in Montmartre that perfectly captures the cinematic neighbourhood.

Meet at the Mysterious Photo Booth

Draw back the curtain of the vintage photo booth at **No. 53 *rue des Trois Frères***. Perhaps you just missed her. If you're carrying spare change, have your photo taken, tear one off the sheet, and scribble 'Don't be a Tourist' on the back. Hide it somewhere in the booth for a stranger to find – and of course, check if someone else reading this book has left one behind for you.

Au Marché de la Butte

A few doors down at the corner, stop in at Amélie's local grocery store, **Au Marché de la Butte**, which still sells fresh market produce and foodstuffs, just as it always did before finding fame on the big screen. You're also certain to find a few souvenirs in honour of Mlle Poulain at the counter.
(*56 rue des Trois Frères, 18ème; open every day, 9am-11pm*)

Continue west, up the *rue des Trois Frères*, past the old-world bistros, pausing at the corner of *rue Ravignan* to take in the view over Paris from the terrace of *Le Relais de La Butte*. Behind the café tables and up the steps is *Place Emile Goudeau*, where Picasso kept a studio at the famous artists' squat **Le Bateau Lavoir**. Only the façade remains, after a fire destroyed most of the building in 1970, but it's a charming shaded spot to sit on a bench and watch the world go by for a moment. Hopefully the local banjo player will be there to play you a song. Continue on down the same road we were headed, which now takes on a second name, *rue Garreau*, and then a third name at the following junction, becoming *rue Durantin*. One of my favourite doors of Paris is at No. 20; also take a look at that exquisite mosaic façade at No. 26 belonging to an old boulangerie, now home to a children's crèche.

Le Petit Moulin

Welcome Home to the Little Windmill

At the end of the block, stop for a drink at the tiny red bar on the corner, **Le Petit Moulin**. They have a small but delicious homemade *Menu du Jour* for €12. It's all handwritten, the ingredients are fresh and organic, and you'll be well looked after by the friendly waitress. If it's cold out, make sure to order the house *vin chaud* (mulled wine).
(*17 rue Tholozé, 18ème; +33 1 80 06 56 82; open every day except Wed, 12.10pm-1am*)

The Scene-Stealing Courtyard

After a heart-warming Montmartre meal, take a look around the back of the restaurant and spy the tall archway at **No. 40 *rue Durantin***. Go and see what lies behind the gate...

Isn't she a beauty? Once known as La Cour aux Juifs (Courtyard of the Jewish), until the 1940s this private residence was inhabited by a local Jewish community. However, when the Nazis conducted their merciless mass arrests of more than 13,000 Parisian Jews in 1941, the courtyard and its surrounding homes were suddenly left empty and silent. If you want to discreetly discover the true beauty of this courtyard up close, wait briefly for a resident to come in or out and they will almost always let you through the gate after them. Just ask respectfully if you can have a look around ('*Je peux jeter un coup d'oeil?*').

Amélie and Dalí go to the Pictures

Back up to *Le Petit Moulin* restaurant and down the *rue Tholozé*. Our last place to find Amélie will be at her favourite little cinema, **Studio 28**, the city's oldest picture house still in operation. In the same room where our Parisian heroine watched movies on Friday nights, wide-eyed and mesmerised, Salvador Dalí premiered his controversial surrealist comedy *L'Âge d'Or* in 1930. The screen was attacked with eggs by audience members of the far right, and the film was banned in France until 1981. If you're not in the mood for a film (although keep in mind they screen the best in French and foreign independent cinema here), there's a bar and secret terrace at the back where you're welcome for a drink. Amélie has to go and pick up her shift now at the **Café des Deux Moulins** down the road

(*15 rue Lepic, 18ème; cafedesdeuxmoulins.fr; open every day until 2am*)

*If you'd like to continue discovering the hidden fairy-tale corners of Montmartre, jump to page 148.

Studio 28

Location Scouting with Woody Allen

Love him or hate him, Woody Allen knows how to make his audience travel back in time. When I think of Woody Allen's Paris, I think of the *rue de la Montagne Sainte-Geneviève* (5ème), where Ernest Hemingway and his buddies pick up Owen Wilson on the steps of the church (St Etienne du Mont) for his nocturnal time travels in *Midnight in Paris*.

Time Travelling at Midnight

If your own Hemingway-driven time machine never comes, work up an appetite rifling through old jazz records at **La Dame Blanche** a few doors down, or at **Croco Jazz** across the cobblestones.
(*47 & 64 rue de la Montagne Sainte-Geneviève, 5ème; both closed Sun*)

La Dame Blanche

With a front-row view of Allen's familiar film set, the terrace of **La Cappanina**, is a no-fuss, light-on-the-pocket Italian restaurant for warm summer evenings. Have a romantic *Lady and the Tramp* moment over some spaghetti, as the chiming of the sunset church bells transports you to another era.
(*64 rue de la Montagne-Sainte-Genevieve, 5ème; call +33 1 43 26 07 42 to secure a table 'en terrasse'*)

On Monday nights, you can indulge in some live gypsy jazz around the corner at **Le Piano Vache**, an atmospheric bar to bring you back to the Quartier Latin of the 1960s.
(*8 rue Laplace, 5ème; +33 1 46 33 75 03; Mon-Sat. See pg. 145 for more jazz spots*)

To finish the evening, lose yourself in the narrow and winding backstreets of the Latin Quarter and make sure to wave to Ernest Hemingway's old window at 74 *rue du Cardinal Lemoine*, his Parisian homestay in the 1920s.

Passage du Grand Cerf

Tunnels to the Belle Époque

Perhaps like another of Allen's *Midnight in Paris* characters, you yearn for a different 'Golden Age' of Paris – the Belle Époque. Travel even further back in time to the 1890s through the city's hidden network of covered passageways, built by visionary architects of the era to provide refuge from the bustling streets of Paris. Lined with elegant shops, fashionable eateries, small theatres, reading rooms and even public baths, they were the stomping ground of the elegant urban dandies and the place to see and be seen before they were replaced by the modern department stores. Today, under the very same antique glass roofs, the small arcade shops have maintained their merchant spirit, selling rare books, old photographs and vintage bric-a-brac. Ideal for rainy weather, instead of taking cover inside modern, soulless department stores, why not try navigating the nostalgic network of covered passages.

Start at *Passage Verdeau* in the 9th arrondissement, which leads to the animated *Passage Jouffroy*. Look out for a miniature furniture shop, Pain d'Epices, and one of the most improbable little hotels in Paris, the Hôtel Chopin. Then cross straight over the busy intersection of the *boulevard Montmartre* into **Passage des Panoramas**, the oldest of the seventeen arcades in Paris to have survived Haussmann's urban regeneration of the mid-1800s. It's now a haven for stamp and vintage postcard collectors, and home to a very good wine bar, Coinstot Vino (pg. 128), and Philippe Starck's Caffè Stern (pg. 80). You'll find an exit at the other end on *rue Saint-Marc*; to your right head south down the *rue Vivienne* for a few minutes until you find the **Galerie Vivienne**, the grandest and most beautifully preserved of the Parisian arcades. At the start of the passage, to the left of the entrance, discover the old map shop, an unmarked boutique filled with rare antique cartography. If the rain lets up, take a ten-minute walk east, where the *Passage du Grand Cerf* awaits. Look up and marvel at the balconies and bridges overhead, where some very lucky Parisians get to reside under the seventeenth-century glass roof.

One of the Last Cinema Prop Houses in Paris

Nestled in the backstreets of Bastille, an improbable place awaits behind a façade of shuttered windows. A family owned business since the 1930s, **Lanzani** is the largest prop house for cinema and theatre in Paris, with thousands and thousands of objects to make believe with. In this endless Aladdin's cave of set dressing, one can roam through aisles and aisles of old-world furniture, wondering which pieces might have been used in what movies, and if that newspaper kiosk wasn't the same one you saw in an old Jean-Luc Godard film. With any luck, you'll run into Wes Anderson in the taxidermy rooms (he keeps a home in Paris and prefers decorating his own sets).

In the main stairwell, you'll meet the house parrot, a resident neotropical macaw who likes to show off by sliding down the banister and nipping at visitors' coats as they walk by. Most prop houses like this have long since moved to affordable spaces in the suburbs, and there are in fact only three left in the city, all located on the same block of streets (one just next door), working together in some capacity to stay afloat. Our prop house does, however, remain a place of business and simply could not cater to a steady stream of curious drop-ins wandering around thanks to me. Having said that, the doors are open, so pop your head in and explore the courtyard full of incredible pieces. More than that and you'd better get in touch with them to make an appointment. If you're an industry professional interested in hiring out props or accessories, you shouldn't have any problem.

(19 rue Basfroi, 11ème; gaetanlanzani.com; by appointment only, Mon- Fri, 8.30am-5.30pm; closes for lunch)

Lanzani

Marché Paul Bert

Brunch-Time at Les Puces

On a crisp sunny Sunday, there really is no better place to be in Paris than **les Puces (the flea market) of Saint-Ouen**. The epicentre of authentic Paris, *le Marché aux Puces de Saint-Ouen* is an ideal little society of its own, made up of fifteen smaller markets, each with their own unique, village-like ambience, preserved by an intellectual and cultivated community of vendors who make it all happen. Les Puces has stories – well-travelled ones – scandalous prices and secret bargains, armchairs sat on by bottoms from every era, clocks that stopped over a hundred years ago, and then, of course, there are the tables ... and I'm not talking about the ones for sale. I'm talking about the tables with the bottles of red wine, saucisson sec and cassoulets that come out at lunchtime, when neighbouring antique dealers dine together as if they were at home, discuss their latest faraway finds, maybe play a hand of cards, and share gossip from the little brocante town. They pay no mind to the bargain hunters who stroll past them, enviously eyeing up the tasty-looking gatherings and realising it must be lunchtime within les Puces! Hungry? Find Chez Louisette, a secret bistro hidden deep in the flea market, pg. 87.

(*Find my favourite markets within les Puces: Marché Vernaison, Marché Paul Bert, Marché Dauphine along the rue des Rosiers, 93400 St Ouen; Métro: Porte de Clignancourt; Sat- Mon*)

Dance your way back to the 1930s

At the end of a paved courtyard sits the **Georges et Rosy** dance school, a veritable time capsule from 1930, founded by a couple who both shared a love for the art of ballroom dancing. International ballroom champions in 1934, their trophy shelf still sits proudly at the entrance, a tribute to their passion and the golden age of dance. In its heyday, nearly a hundred people would fill this little dance school nightly. Parisians flocked to get their chance to dance and learn alongside Georges and Rosy, and indeed, a diverse range of familiar names have danced within these walls, including Edith Piaf, Karl Lagerfeld, Kristin Scott Thomas and even President Charles de Gaulle.

The original parquet dance floor is surrounded by large mirrors, creating an illusion of a grandiose ballroom, and little white tables and chairs sit on the sidelines. In the cloakroom, old wood-stained boxes are stacked above the coat rack; each one has a name and contains a pair of dance shoes belonging to a regular at the school, or to one from a generation before them. Nothing seems to have changed here for nearly ninety years.

When the couple passed in 1985, a former student at the school took over and carried on their legacy by managing the intimate academy. Roland's heart and soul lies within these walls. Whether you're a beginner or a professional, he welcomes new students at all levels. With his English teaching assistant, Lucy, they offer tango classes, slow foxtrot, jive, samba, cha-cha and the Viennese Valse, all of which can be taught one-to-one during the day or in a small evening class. Pop by on a Friday evening when the school holds a mini soirée after class with wine and nibbles. If you fancy trying something new, or perhaps you used to dance and wish to reignite an old passion, Georges et Rosy offers more than a place to learn a few steps. It's a chance to step back to a time when asking someone to dance wasn't such a rarity.

(*20 rue de Varennes, 7ème; +33 1 45 48 66 76; Mon-Sat, 10am-10pm; €10 one-off entry Fri evening; timetables and prices on georgesetrosy.com*)

Waiting for Bardot

In the 1960s, Brigitte Bardot made everyone wish they were French. She's better known for gallivanting around St Tropez in short shorts, but the French film actress was born and raised in Paris, where she began her career in show business at the age of fifteen and later became the muse of French music legend Serge Gainsbourg.

Brigitte Bardot on the set of *Come dance with me!* in 1959.

The BB Club

Brigitte, famously nicknamed 'BB' by Gainsbourg, began a passionate affair with the legendary musician, who also launched her singing career. They were both regulars at a restaurant and nightclub called **Castel**; located in a small backstreet of Saint-Sulpice in the 6th arrondissement, it is one of the few Parisian hotspots of her day that has stood the test of time. After a slump in the '90s, Castel made a comeback recently, with modern-day Bardot types once again disappearing behind the lipstick red façade into a three-storey relic of 1960s Parisian nightlife. Mick Jagger, who once fell for Françoise Hardy in the lavish nightspot, came back for the re-opening, and Gainsbourg's piano now sits in the fumoir. Book dinner at the restaurant to avoid any 'members only' hassle at the door, but dress to impress.

(*15 rue Princesse, 6ème; restaurant reservations: +33 1 40 51 52 80*)

Chez Nenesse

To soothe a hangover and escape the groupies and the paparazzi, I've always imagined Brigitte at a place like **Chez Nenesse**, a real local family-run bistro (like they used to be). Like somewhere straight off a French film set, with red chequered tablecloths and black-and-white tiled flooring, everything here is prepared by an elderly husband and wife team, M. et Mme Leplu.

(*17 rue de Saintonge, 3ème; +33 1 42 78 46 49*)

Swinging Sixties Style

After lunch and too many cigarettes, let's say Brigitte might have had a fitting with her favourite French designer, Pierre Cardin, who conveniently has a museum nearby that sends you on a blast through the past of swinging '60s fashion. **Museé Pierre Cardin** is filled with an army of mannequins dressed in his most iconic outfits. If you appreciate vintage fashion, it's a fantastic feast for the eyes.

(*5 rue Saint-Merri, 4ème; pierrecardin.com/museum; Wed-Fri, 11am-6pm; Sat-Sun, 1pm-6pm*)

Queen of the Mods

Oh-so *Twin Peaks*, with its red velvet curtains, neon lighting and surreal decoration around the bar, **La Coquille** is a neighbourhood drinking den for a local clientele that is stuck in a bit of a time warp from when Bardot was queen of the Parisian mods. You'll meet all sorts of characters in here, and certainly have a few strange encounters, but a late-night whiskey will transport you back to BB's Paris.

(*30 rue Coquillière, 1er, Mon-Sat, 9am-1.30am*)

Audrey Hepburn Classics

'Paris is always a good idea,' she said in *Sabrina*. The city that Audrey Hepburn gave us on screen is an elegant, smart and perfect Paris, and sometimes, it's just what I feel like...

A Hepburn-Worthy Lunch Scene

If **Chez Julien** had been around in Audrey Hepburn's day, there would no doubt be a movie still of her sitting on the terrace in a matching blue Dior dress. The former nineteenth-century boulangerie turned restaurant is spot on for a candlelit evening with truffled foie gras, or a cinematic brunch outside. On sunny days, call ahead or go early to get a table on the terrace, with its postcard view of the old Saint-Gervais church.

(*1 rue du Pont Louis-Philippe, 4ème; +33 1 42 78 31 64*)

Postcards from *Sabrina*

In my opinion, there was something desperately lacking in Hepburn and Bogart's 1954 classic, *Sabrina*. Where was the sequence à la *Pretty Woman* showing her Parisian transformation from girl next door to sophisticated style queen? It's as if they skipped over what should have been the best scene of the film! So let's imagine the shopping trip that should have made movie montage history. Start by ducking into the **Village Royale** (also known as the Cité Berryer), a hidden oasis of retail therapy where some of the fanciest fashion houses of Paris have set up shop in what used to be an eighteenth-century food market. The likes of Chanel and Dior have become the new butcher shops and fishmongers, but this picturesque shopping alley has nevertheless kept the charm of yesteryear.

(*Find the entrance to Village Royale at 25 rue Royale, 8ème; villageroyal.com*)

The Little Black Dress

I always think of Audrey when I'm in the nearby elegant gardens and covered marble arcades of the *Palais Royale*, a seventeenth-century royal enclave sealed

off from the busy boulevards near the Louvre. Beneath the fluted pilasters and Corinthian capitals, alongside flower beds and trickling water fountains, browse the time-capsule boutiques that still have their artisanal shop signs from a hundred years ago. It just so happens that one of these boutiques is a vintage store dedicated entirely to the 'little black dress', the wardrobe staple that became a Hollywood icon in its own right thanks to Hepburn. The window of **La Petite Robe Noir** is filled with exquisite black dresses, each with its own story, curated by the king of vintage *haute couture*, **Didier Ludot**. Stroll to the other side of the courtyard and you'll find his original vintage store selling perfect-condition pieces from every decade – an Yves Saint Laurent suit from the '70s or a Chanel jacket from the '50s.

(*24 Galerie Montpensier, Jardin du Palais Royal, 1er; didierludot.fr; Mon-Sat, 10.30am-7pm*)

Act like you're wearing Givenchy

If you happen to have the budget for a red 1950s Givenchy dress with a matching chiffon scarf, just like the one Audrey was wearing as she frolicked about in front of the 'Venus de Milo' for that epic scene at the Louvre in *Funny Face* – well, you'll probably need somewhere to wear it, right? Givenchy or not, sometimes a dress just needs a place worthy of re-enacting a classic Hepburn moment. Most passers-by have no idea you can dine in al fresco splendour behind the gigantic columns of the Grand Palais museum. The entrance to the restaurant, called the **Mini Palais**, is sort of tucked away at the side entrance of the museum, and at night its magnificent terrace is bathed in glorious red lighting (to match that red dress). This hidden gem is also open for tea and cakes in between mealtimes – a much-needed afternoon haven away from the Champs-Élysées. On your way to the *toilettes*, find the door with a little window where you can peek through to the famous glass-domed gallery of the Grand Palais.

(*At the corner of Cours la Reine & avenue Winston Churchill, 8ème; +33 1 42 56 42 42; every day, 10am-2am*)

Place d' Hepburn

If I were to choose one spot in Paris that most embodies the elegance of Audrey Hepburn, I wouldn't hesitate to choose the ***Place de Furstenberg***, a petite Left Bank oasis that you wouldn't find if you didn't go looking for it. Enter this square and travel back to 1950s Saint-Germain, where Audrey first dined with Hubert de Givenchy in a nearby restaurant and convinced him to design the costumes for *Sabrina*, winning him over with stories of her childhood as a dancer. You can imagine them strolling through the *Place de Furstenberg* after dinner, arm in arm. Maybe it's the roundabout's statuesque five-globe streetlight that looks like a ballerina centre stage, or the perfectly monochrome colour palette that reminds me of her little black dresses, but I do declare that they should have just renamed it *Place de Hepburn*. While you're there, have a wander around the former **painter's studio of Eugène Delacroix**, once neighbour to Claude Monet, who kept the studio upstairs.

(*Musée National Eugène Delacroix, 6 rue de Furstenberg, 6ème; 9.30am-5.30pm, closed Tues*)

Left: Le Pure Café
Previous: Village Royale

Date Night

Cool & Casual

1   Remember Ethan Hawke and Julie Delpy's Parisian date discussing love and life in *Before Sunset*? Tell me you didn't miss out on the movie that perfectly shows off the real charm of this city (it's actually one of the few Hollywood films set in Paris where we don't see the Eiffel Tower). They filmed the café scene at **Le Pure Café**, which has that local bohemian bistro vibe; a vintage zinc bar, an easy-going barman, and a regular clientele (but never overcrowded). Classic but not cliché, it's perfect for a laid-back and uncomplicated coffee date.
(*14 rue Jean Macé, 11ème; lepurecafe.fr; open every day, 7am-1am*)

2   **Verjus Wine Bar** is a welcoming little vino cave with flattering mood lighting and no formal seating – just pull up a stool at the counter and order some heavenly sharing plates from around €4-€7 each and interesting wines to sample at €5-€12 a glass. If at any point you want to upgrade the date, check if they have a table upstairs in the main restaurant, where things get a little more

serious (and pricey), with a set tasting menu and wine pairings – a formula that usually sounds stuffy, but not here. The food at Verjus is a total aphrodisiac. (*47 rue de Montpensier, 1er; open Mon- Fri, 6pm-11pm; no reservations. For the restaurant, reserve at verjusparis.com*)

3   Dating on the down-low? For a seriously discreet rendezvous, head to **Le Bar**, on a quiet residential street in the heart of the 6th arrondissement. Ring the bell to escape the outside world and gain entry to a dimly lit velvet lounge with opium-den inspired decorative accents. An encyclopaedic selection of spirits compliments the very mysterious but relaxing ambience. Cocktails are served one way only: strong. (*27 rue de Condé, 5ème; +33 1 43 29 06 61; Tues-Sat, 9pm to 3am/4am*)

4   You'll walk into **Floyd's** from the street entrance and assume it's another moody craft cocktail bar with taxidermy on the wall, but a surprise awaits you all the way in the back, past the sweet-smelling kitchen cooking up all kinds of irresistible delights. Discover the bar's hidden alter ego, a beautiful restaurant with a Palm Springs vibe and chic loft-style decor. A talented American in Paris, Jamie Young, is the Bostonian chef behind the Franco-American fusion menu that includes buffalo frog's legs. Not to scare you off – there are some classic steakhouse plates on the menu too, as well as a perfect aphrodisiac: the Oysters Rockefeller. (*11 rue d'Enghien, 10ème; + 33 1 44 79 05 52; Tues-Sun for lunch and dinner, Sat dinner only*)

Classic Casanova

1   A nineteenth-century poet once described the *Place Dauphine* as the 'vagina of Paris', because of its erotic triangular V shape. Rumour has it King Henri IV modelled it after the private parts of his favourite courtesan. Ah, French romance. Vaginas aside, it is one of my favourite squares in Paris, tucked away on an island in the middle of the Seine. Book a table at the **Caveau du Palais**, but stress that your table must be outside (*'en terrasse'*), overlooking the sandy gravel square with locals playing pétanques and some of Paris's most beautiful townhouses in the background. It's the cherry on the cake. Just maybe don't crack any vagina jokes if this is a first date. (*17-19 Place Dauphine, 1er; +33 1 43 26 04 28; open every day for lunch and dinner*)

2   I once heard **La Petrelle** is where French presidents take their mistresses. The windows are veiled with curtains hung just high enough so as not to give anything away about what or who is inside. La Petrelle has been around for more than twenty years, run by a sort of mad-hatter Frenchman, Jean-Luc André. It is a true cabinet of curiosities that will win the heart of any visitor with a weakness for collecting the bizarre things of this world. Surrounded

by piles of books and curious objects you might unearth in your eccentric grandparent's attic, you'll have to take your time deciphering the menu, which is handwritten by Jean-Luc in his wild scribbling penmanship. It's like reading a love letter about food. In keeping with the cluttered decor of the restaurant, the food doesn't come neatly or pretentiously arranged on a plate – it's all a bit of a beautiful French mess. The freshest produce is infused with the kind of sauces a grandmother would only pass down to her favourite grandchild. Don't expect to find your average bottle of grape juice here; the owner gets his wines at auctions and your cheapest red comes at around €30. La Petrelle is for special occasions; a treat for the very important person in your life.
(*34 rue Petrelle; 9ème; +33 1 42 82 11 02; Tues-Sat*)

3   In Saint-Germain, there's a special *epicerie* (grocery shop) open until the stroke of midnight that is perfect for switching up a wimpish picnic date on the Seine. Show your appreciation for good, authentic French produce and meet up with your date at **L'epicerie Oliver Piton** on a warm summer's eve. Pick out some late-night gourmet picnic plates together from the fresh cold-cuts bar and the divine cake display (they've got the wine and cheese covered too), before strolling over to the banks of the river at the end of the street.
(*23 rue des Saints-Pères, 6ème; open every day until midnight*)

La Petrelle

Creative

1   **Tango Dancing on the Seine**. As long as the weather is good, tango enthusiasts, advanced and never-before-danced, gather at the mini amphitheatres along the Seine in the 5th arrondissement, to tango until twilight. A little old man sits on the edge of the river with his radio playing Argentinian accordion music and guarding the dancers' belongings. If you're too shy to join in, sitting with a bottle

Jardin des Serres d'Auteuil

of wine on the steps and watching these dancers is still absolutely mesmerising and incredibly romantic. Spectators watch quietly, listening to the dragging of tango feet on the stone banks. It's people-watching with a very sexy twist. (*Square Tino Rossi, Quai St Bernard, 5ème; Wed-Sun from 8.30pm. There are free tango classes with Ray and Eric from 7pm. On the same riverbank, there are also stages for salsa dancing and 1950s jiving*)

2   Pack a baguette, some runny cheese and a bottle of wine and grab the table waiting for you in sub-tropical temperatures under the biggest palm tree in Paris. You're taking your date for a greenhouse picnic. Entry to the eighteenth-century indoor botanical garden, **Jardin des Serres d'Auteuil**, is absolutely free just open the door and step into summer. You won't have to fight anyone for a seat at your picnic in paradise – even on weekends there's hardly anyone there. Perfect for getting lost in the jungle, there are several greenhouses to dip in and out of, changing to various hotter and milder temperatures according to the type of plants growing inside. The largest one, with the giant palm tree, has a few garden tables for the dreamiest summer picnics, even in the depths of winter. The tropical birds will provide the soundtrack.
(*3 avenue de la Porte d'Auteuil, 16ème; open every day, 9am-7.30pm*)

3   You're sat holding a pink balloon at a spot you chose along the banks of the Canal Saint-Martin. You were given said balloon by **Pink Flamingo**, a pizza parlour around the corner, whose bicycle delivery man uses it as a beacon to locate you and present you with your order – a pie reminiscent of some of the best New York-style slices.
(*67 rue Bichat, 10ème; +33 1 42 02 31 70*)

Crazy in Love

1   **L'Hotel**, the intimate and discreet boutique hotel where Oscar Wilde lived and died, hides a very special secret. Behind heavy velvet curtains, at the bottom of a winding stone staircase, a medieval undercroft sets the scene for a private swim in the **Piscine Hamman**. From Tuesday to Saturday, you can reserve this stunning candlelit pool all to yourself. It comes with a hefty price tag, as you might have guessed; for €200, the *après-midi detente* package allows you two hours at the spa, with toe massages, champagne, tea and pastries.
(*13 rues des Beaux-Arts, 6ème; +33 1 44 41 99 00; l-hotel.com*)

2   During the Belle Époque, there was a restaurant on the river that catered specifically to married gentlemen who wanted to discreetly entertain Parisian courtesans with champagne and expensive gifts. The owner installed lavish private rooms for his patrons and the restaurant instantly became an institution. The private rooms of **Lapernouse**, open since 1776, are still there

today. Ask to reserve 'La Belle Otero' (it's the cosiest) and impress your date with a little trivia about the restaurant's antique mirrors, which still bear the scratches from courtesans testing their lovers' diamond gifts on the glass to verify their authenticity.

(*51 Quai des Grands Augustins, 6ème; +33 1 43 26 68 04; Mon-Sat*)

3   If you feel like a particularly good sunset might be coming on, there's a special place to make a bee-line for with your significant other. **The Temple of Love**, a.k.a. *le Temple Romantique*, sits on an island in the middle of a lake in the Bois de Vincennes, the largest public park in the city. It requires a little bit of a field trip from the very centre of Paris, but adventure dates are always the best kind. Hop on the line 8 métro and hop off at the stop Michel Bizot. Walk up the palm-tree-lined avenue until you reach the Lac Daumesnil (that's the lake) and spot the Temple of Love from the shore. You can access the island, Île de Reuilly, by footbridge, but I suggest you rent a little rowboat to get across; each has its own name, so if you manage to nab one with your love's name written on it, you've basically got this in the bag.

If you're planning to pop the question at the Temple of Love (*congratulations!*), the divine Rococo temple and the views over the lake won't disappoint, and don't forget to discover what's *beneath* the temple. To the left of the stone kiosk you'll find a rocky stairway down to the shore of the lake, where a secret grotto awaits.

(*Temple Romantique, Île de Reuilly; 12ème*)

Le Temple Romantique

Perfect for Popping the Question

1   Are your stars aligned? Get this: on Monday and Friday evenings you can visit
the **Sorbonne Observatory**, where they used to teach astronomy to university
students over a century ago. Under a wooden dome, 40 metres above the city,
all the observatory equipment dates back to the 1930s, including the impressive
telescope, which still works perfectly. The enchanting tour comes complete
with stargazing from the panoramic balcony that boasts breath-taking views
of Paris. There are just five spots available per visit and the only way to make
an appointment is to call this number (+33 1 42 24 13 74), write a cheque for €7
to Société Astronomique de France, and send it to 3 *rue Beethoven*, 75016, Paris.
There can sometimes be a waiting list of several months, which only makes it all
the more special, of course.
(*17 rue de la Sorbonne, 5ème*)

2   Nestled at the end of a tree-lined pathway, a garden of bellflowers, lilacs and
wisteria is thriving happily at la **Musée de la Vie Romantique**. The private
townhouse that once entertained the likes of Delacroix, Chopin and Rossini has
been a museum devoted to the Romantic Movement in the arts since 1981. From
mid-March to mid-October, an old glasshouse next to the main house is home
to a charming tea room serving lunch and Egyptian iced tea made with hibiscus
flowers and cinnamon. On a sun-drenched afternoon, it's simply paradise.
(*16 rue Chaptal, 9ème; museevieromantique.paris.fr; Tues-Sun, 10am-6pm*)

Musée de la Vie Romantique

#DBTParis 📷

I owe so many of my Paris discoveries to Instagram. When I first arrived in Paris I started following all the local accounts I could find to help me get to know the city better. So I thought maybe now we could start our own Instagram trail to help travellers scout for curious and nostalgic places of note. Perhaps you have a thing for unusual Parisian doors, ghost signs, tiny shops or hidden courtyards. Let's you and I trade Paris secrets using the hashtag #**DBTParis** (DBT, as in, *Don't Be a Tourist*).

To get us started, I'll let you in on a few of my most Instagrammable spots to track down. When you find them, snap a photo and use the #DBTParis hashtag to update our little club on any news or changes to the location. See you on Instagram!

Charming Shopfronts

Olympia Le Tan: The accessories designer inspired by classic literature has a most charming dollhouse boutique hidden behind the Palais Royal.
(*Passage des Deux Pavillons, 5 rue des Petits Champs, 1er; closed Sun*)

Boot Cafe: A tiny old shoe repair shop converted, but not necessarily updated, to a coffee shop in the Marais.
(*19 rue du Pont aux Choux, 3ème; open every day, 10am–6pm*)

Beaurepaire Café: A setting I can never tire of for a glass of wine. Candlelit tables, string lights on a quiet square behind the Seine; it's simply a movie scene.
(*1 rue de la Bûcherie, 5ème; closed Mon*)

Herboristerie de la Place de Clichy: The oldest and most famous herbalist in Paris and a treasure trove of healing magical potions.
(*87 rue d'Amsterdam, 8ème; Mon–Sat, closes for lunch*)

Hôtel Chopin: A small hotel straight out of an Agatha Christie novel, the façade of old-world typography awaits at the end of one of Paris's hidden passages of the Belle Époque.
(*46 Passage Jouffroy, 9ème*)

Boulangerie Boris Lumé: A patisserie so picture-perfect even Meryl Streep filmed a scene here for *Julie & Julia*.
(*48 rue Caulaincourt, 18ème; closed Mon*)

Marilyn Institut: A candy-pink beauty parlour out of time.
(*2 rue de Constance, 18ème*)

L'Objet qui Parle: The owner of this charming little antiques shop treats his front window like an art installation, full of curious objects that will really speak to you.
(*86 rue des Martyrs; 18ème; open 1pm–7.30pm, closed Mon*)

Left: L'Objet qui Parle

Overleaf: Passage de l'Ancre

Insta-Ready Streets

- *Rue Legouvé*: You can see there was once a building in between the two red-brick walls on either side of the street. Don't miss the old public bathhouse. (*10ème*)
- *Rue Sainte-Marthe*: A rainbow of old shopfronts turned into residential homes. Enjoy the Provençale oasis at the end of the street, on *Place Sainte-Marthe*. (*10ème*)
- *Rue Crémieux*: My 'little Portobello' in Paris. (*11ème*)
- *Impasse Marie Blanche*: Look for the ghost brocante and the mysterious gothic mansion at the end of the road. (*18ème*)
- *Villa Leandre*: The prettiest cottages of Montmartre. (*18ème*)
- *Villa de l'Ermitage*: A leafy urban hamlet complete with a shared vegetable garden. Find the entry point at 315 *rue des Pyrenees*. (*20ème*)

Behind the Façades

Passage de l'Ancre: A delightful passageway hidden in the heart of the Marais. Look out for the old umbrella shop and the anchor-shaped sign of an old hostel at the end of the street, hence the name 'ancre'.
(*Enter via 223 rue Saint-Martin, 3ème*)

14 rue Amélie: Behind the concrete garage driveway, you'll find a charming country cottage with the most unexpected view of the Eiffel Tower.
(*7ème*)

Avenue Frochot: Behind the gates of one of Paris's most secretive addresses, you'll find a hidden hamlet of neo-Renaissance villas, wisteria trees and rose bushes. The nineteenth-century villa at No. 1 is said to be haunted and mansion No. 4 was home to a famous bohemian courtisan called La Présidente. Marked by the elaborate stained glass window of an old 1930s cabaret to the left of the entrance, *avenue Frochot* is closed to the public, but if you can muster up the courage to kindly ask a passing resident to follow them behind the iron gates, pretend to belong and wander without disturbing its peace.
(*9ème*)

Cité Napoleon: Enter discreetly without the door code (on weekdays only) to discover a maze of apartments under a glass roof, built circa 1851; the city's first attempt to create housing for the working classes.
(*Rue Rochechouart, 9ème*)

Passage l'Homme: For the atelier ghost signs.
(*Find it at 26 rue Charonne, 11ème*)

Villa des Platanes: You can tell from the impressive iron gates on the boulevard that something pretty special awaits on the other side. If you're patient enough, with a bit of luck you can get inside to see this stunning courtyard, with its grand staircases and statues.
(*58 boulevard Clichy, 18ème*)

Cité du Midi: Look up for that rusty old ghost sign that reads '*Bains*'. Did you know that until as recently as the 1960s, only one out of five Parisian apartments had bathing facilities?
(*48 boulevard du Clichy, 18ème*)

13 rue Germain-Pilon: When in Montmartre, go hunting for this private townhouse and get a peek of its mysterious underpass beneath the entryway. It's basically a life goal of mine to squeeze through the railings and get to the other side of that tunnel.
(*18ème*)

PS Find me on Instagram @messynessychic

Romantic Markets

Locals hauling around their grocery baskets, market vendors doing their theatrics, the smell of onion galettes wrapping around me – French food markets make my heart swell. I'll never tire of these moveable feasts. Repeat every day at a different market for best results...

Fancy Fast Food

Every Saturday morning at the **Marché avenue du President Wilson**, you'll find the Parisian bourgeoisie dragging their caddies and straw bags full of fresh gourmet produce up and down the stalls. This one fights for the title of the city's poshest food market, catering to the sort of local clientele that's looking for only the best foie gras to serve their dinner party guests. The fishmongers, the butchers, the cheesemongers, the fruit and legume sellers, even the guys roasting the chickens on a spit – all are masters of their craft. Speaking of chicken, ask the rotisserie boys to bag you one of their baby chickens called a *coquelet*, which makes a hearty lunch for one and a perfect snack for two. Take it to the banks of the Seine and eat the entire thing with your fingers from the bag. That is what I call Parisian fast food.
(*Avenue du Président Wilson, 16ème; +33 1 45 11 71 11; Wed & Sat, 7am-2.30pm*)

Drunken Sandwiches

Blink and you'll miss the iron gates to the **Marché des Enfants Rouge**, one of the oldest and most hidden markets in Paris, tucked away in the less touristy, more trendy part of the *Marais*, which Parisians now call the *Haut Marais*. For lunch, this place is a hungry traveller's paradise. You can choose from French roasts, Moroccan delights, runny cheeses, and salty charcuterie, and devour it all at communal tables surrounding the market stalls. And then there is Alain, the most imaginative sandwich-maker in Paris. He may be slightly mad, and you'll probably never see him without a glass of red wine within reach, but his galette/crêpe sandwiches are the stuff of legend. His *Cornet Végétarien*, filled with fresh avocado, chêvre, honey, persil and secret spices, is pure poetry in a sandwich. When you're done, pick up some fresh market flowers and take a stroll down the nearby *rue Houdon* to browse the small fashion boutiques.
(*39 rue de Bretagne, 3ème; +33 1 40 11 20 40, open every day*)

The Century-Old Wholefoods

If you're looking for organic (think trays of fresh wheatgrass), the **Marché Biologique Raspail** will have what you're looking for on Sundays. It's unlikely that you'll be able to resist the scent of potato onion pancakes, lentil tarts and baked goods, and the variety of seafood is something you'd expect to see at a seaside port. Be prepared to burn a hole in your pocket, but you'll find smiles all

around at this friendly farmers' market – and look out for French screen legend Catherine Deneuve coming to buy her weekly groceries.
(*Boulevard Raspail, 6ème; Métro: Notre-Dame des Champs; Sun, 9am-3pm*)

The Indoor Neighbourhood Market
Marché Beauvau is a beautiful covered market within an outdoor section near Bastille offering a diverse smorgasbord of foods from the Basque Country to North Africa. You'll find lower prices and more locals at this market, as well as a small flea market on the square.
(*Place d'Aligre; 12ème; +33 1 14 51 17 11; open mornings and 4pm-7.30pm, closed Mon*)

10 Paris Movies to get you in the Mood

1   *Funny Face* (1957)
2   *A Bout de Souffle* ('Breathless', 1960)
3   *Amélie* (2001)
4   *The Dreamers* (2003)
5   *Paris, je t'aime* (2006)
6   *2 Days in Paris* (2007)
7   *Gainsbourg* (2010)
8   *Hugo* (2011)
9   *Midnight in Paris* (2011)
10   *As Above, So Below* (2014)

Palaeontology gallery
at the Muséum National
d'Histoire Naturelle

03

Anywhere but the Louvre

Hi Nessy,

Firstly, thank you for listing your email so bravely for random people like me to contact you. I'm a chef in my twenties, living in Brooklyn, and had one of those 'I need to get the hell out of here or I'll go crazy' moments and decided to book a trip to Paris. Like you, I have an abhorrence of touristy things and prefer the unknown. The thought of walking around the Louvre has little appeal for me and I think I'd rather be punched in the face than take a guided tour. How can I get an authentic cultural experience in the city, avoiding queues and guided tours, without feeling like I've missed the important stuff?
    Cheers!

From Kristen,
an American Chef

I generally avoid the Louvre. How can you stop and appreciate art in such touristy chaos? And have you seen how tiny the 'Mona Lisa' really is? This city has so many other ways to get your culture fix, so let's leave all those people to queue for hours while we start with a hidden Paris archive just a few streets away...

Underrated Museums

My Hidden Paris Archive

We're on the hunt for **La Galcante**, a clever little French portmanteau combining *galerie* and *brocante*. Look for the big blue door on *rue de l'Abre Sec*, where a trolley of old books will lure the wandering eye. Dip into the passageway, enter a peaceful cobblestone courtyard and give a firm push to the rickety old doors, letting the aroma of ageing print curl around you. It's the scent of more than 7 million copies of various newspapers, magazines and affairs of the press dating as far back as the old French Regime of the fifteenth century. The faint sound of classical jazz comes from a radio in a back room, where a woman's voice calls out, *'Entrez, entrez! J'arrive.'* That's Juliette. She won't be out for a while and prefers to leave you to it until you need something. Begin your side-stepping dance through narrow aisles of paper piled high, skimming your fingers over the tops of rare and out-of-print magazines.

La Galcante

You can probably find every copy of *Le Monde* ever printed, but they also have a vast collection of international print, including an impressive stash of *The New Yorker* magazine dating back to the early 1960s, all in very good condition. But La Galcante isn't just a place to find yesterday's news. Dig through eye-catching collectable trinkets and pore over beautiful vintage maps outlining countries that no longer exist. Juliette will lead you into a dusty back room if you're looking for something really particular. With a cigarette hanging out of the corner of her mouth, rambling on about how busy she's been all day, she climbs up a ladder and disappears behind the boxes on the mezzanine, assuring you that you should never come up here because the floor is about to cave in. She smokes and swears and complains a lot, but she knows every last inch of this archive, back to front. As you close the door of La Galcante behind you with a rattle, clutching a twenty-five-year-old souvenir in a brown paper bag and admiring the winding staircases of the silent courtyard, give a thought to all those crowds of people who spent most of their afternoon queuing at the Louvre just a few streets over. Our little secret.

(*52 rue de l'Arbre Sec, 1er, lagalcante.com; Mon-Sat, 10am – 7.30pm*)

A Recommendation for Wes Anderson

Behind the terracotta blue doorway to not one, but two seventeenth-century mansions, is la **Musée de la Chasse et de la Nature** (Museum of Hunting and Nature), probably the most underrated museum in the city. Peruse an eclectic antique collection of exotic taxidermy and natural history curios alongside stylish

Musée de la Chasse et de la Nature

contemporary art exhibitions. Have a good rummage through drawers filled with ancient weapons that belonged to fabled warrior kings, then find the collection of ancient gold dog collars displayed alongside a Jeff Koons puppy sculpture. But don't miss the Trophy Room, an artwork in itself, that houses hundreds of taxidermied animals donated by princes and legendary hunting parties from around the world. For every animal on display, you can find its history documented in beautiful card catalogues. The huge amount of respect shown for these beasts allows you to leave your squeamishness at the door and just be in awe. Have this incredible museum almost entirely to yourself for an €8 entry fee. (*62 rue des Archives, 3ème; chassenature.org; Tues-Sun, 11am-6pm & open late Wed until 9.30pm*)

The Ghost of Edith Piaf

Even if you don't know much about Edith Piaf or her music ('*Non, je ne regrette rien*'), you won't regret making time for the **Musée Edith Piaf**. The curious and eccentric little museum is set in a Belleville apartment belonging to Mr Bernard Marchois, a devoted fan of Piaf's since he met her at the age of sixteen. Achieving a sense of intimacy rarely found in museums, Marchois displays Piaf's personal belongings and memorabilia, including private letters, furniture from her apartment, her famous black dresses, books and records, which play softly in the background. It's as if she's just out of sight, in the bedroom applying another layer of eyebrow pencil writing letters to her lost love. (*5 rue Crespin du Gast, 11ème; +33 1 43 55 52 72, call to reserve more than a week in advance; Mon-Wed, 1pm-6pm*)

Jalal's Cave of Music History

The Phono Museum is what a music lover's dream looks like. Hidden in plain sight in the shadow of the Moulin Rouge, there's 140 years of recorded sound history stuffed inside this Aladdin's cave. Every timeworn object in here still plays music perfectly. Just pick any phonograph or music box in the museum's endless collection and have a listen to the sound of a bygone era (often from the same vinyl that the museum acquired it with). You'll be asking yourself: 'Who collected all this stuff? Shouldn't those antique gramophones be behind glass? You can really still play music on that thing? And wait just a damn minute, is that a Swiss chalet dollhouse doubling as a record player?'

Jalal Aro, the man who collected it all, has so much knowledge about the bohemian neighbourhoods in Paris, like Montmartre, which nurtured and accepted black American talent before America did, legitimising jazz for the rest of the world. Jala is also the guy that Woody Allen and Quentin Tarantino come to when they need vintage musical props. With an infectious laugh and his old-school cool-cat style – the leather jacket, flat cap, and the best sideburns I've seen since *Starsky and Hutch* – Jalal is one of those memorable characters

that make up what I like to call the 'Humans of Montmartre'. I believe it's the appreciation of these nostalgic characters and the survival of their eccentric establishments that will keep the true spirit of Montmartre and bygone Paris alive. Don't miss the vintage record store at the back of the museum, **Le Phonogalerie**, filled with rare recordings, antique gramophones and original artwork for sale.

(*10 rue Lallier, 9ème; phonomuseum.fr; Thurs-Sun, 2pm-6pm*)

A Giant Cabinet of Curiosities

Muséum National d'Histoire Naturelle, a.k.a. the Natural History Museum, sounds very 'science class field trip', which is probably why so many tourists miss out on this city's most curious wonderland. Start in the impressive *Grande Galerie* and find the secret south-east corner staircase behind an unassuming doorway in the shadows of a giant blue whale skeleton. The higher up you go, the more it looks like Harry Potter's Hogwarts. The staircases unveil a hidden layer of the building's history, when it was once the king's own cabinet of natural history and an unparalleled scientific institution in the 1700s. Throw open a window at the highest floor for a magnificent view over the gardens and greenhouses, where, depending on the season, giant pumpkins and squash are growing out in the open. You can check how ripe they are on your way to the **Palaeontology Gallery** (*Galeries d'Anatomie comparée et de Paléontologie*), which, again, might sound more suited for a science class field trip, but just trust me. This is hands down the most impressive collection of skeletons you'll ever lay eyes upon. Meet the Noah's ark ghost army in limbo, waiting to march back to the ark, two by two. This gallery hasn't been renovated for over a hundred years – and I hope it stays that way. The walls are peeling and the floorboards are creaking; the paper labels in the cabinets are yellowed from age and the calligraphy is of another time. You can even peek up to the old archives on the top floor and see books covered in dust in forgotten glass bookcases.

(*Jardin des Plantes, 57 rue Cuvier, 5ème; +33 1 40 79 30 00; mnhn.fr*)

Semnopithèque...

Semnopithèque mitré.
Lophopithecus mitratus.
de Sumatra par M. Duvaucel
1.1905

Semnopithèque maure.
Trachypithecus maurus
de Java par M. Diard.
1.1905

Semnopithèque maure.
Trachypithecus maurus
de Java par M. Diard.

Semnopithèque nasique.
Nasalis larvatus.
de Java par M. Diard. 1.1806

Semnopithèque à huppe noire.
Lophopithecus melalophus.
de Sumatra par M. Duvaucel
1.1905

Pubis.   Ischion.

Semnopithèque obscur.   Semnopithèque obscur.   Semnopithèque obscur.
Lophopithecus obscurus.   Lophopithecus obscurus.

Salle d'Armes Coudurier
fencing club

A Time Capsule Fencing Club of Paris

Approaching through the hidden courtyard of **Salle d'Armes Coudurier**, you
begin to hear the sound of tapping metal, sliding and tapping quickly again.
There's a warm glow through the windowpanes of a door marked 'Salle d'Armes';
weapons room. We've found the oldest fencing club in Paris, founded in 1886
during the sport's golden age. At a time when the slightest insult exchanged between
gentlemen would likely end in a duel, fencing schools were all over the city. Up
until World War II, there were at least two fencing clubs per arrondissement in
Paris, but they've been disappearing ever since. Everything has remained intact
inside this club's walls since its creation in the late nineteenth century. Nothing
has changed, except maybe a few tell-tale electric appliances like the telephone circa
1990 and a light-up globe sitting on the desk in the corner. The breastplate of a previous
owner, a General of the Franco-Prussian War, still hangs on the wall. Fulfilling his
childhood dream, Jean-Pierre Pinel La Taule has been the master of the house
since 1971, keeping the name, tradition, honour and teaching just as it was in the
beginning. Open to men, women and children, La Taule's club has students as
young as seven who practise on Wednesday evenings, reserved for beginners,
but there is no age limit, young or old. Newcomers can attend on any day for a
trial class. A membership costs €57 a month.
(*6 rue Git-le-Cœur, 6ème; call + 33 1 43 54 49 97 for a trial class; open Mon-Sat, 5pm-
9pm*)

Snooping Around Other People's Houses

They used to be someone's private home, now they're open as small time-
capsule museums:

Musée Gustave Moreau, for his steampunk staircase.
(*14 rue de la Rochefoucauld, 9ème; musee-moreau.fr; closed Tues*)
Musée Jacquemart André, for the winter garden, an exotic vestibule under a
glass ceiling designed by the world-travelling couple who once lived there.

(*158 boulevard Haussmann, 8ème; musee-jacquemart-andre.com; open every day*)

Musée Zadkine, to hang out in the prettiest and most tranquil artist's atelier in Paris.

(*100bis rue d'Assas, 6ème; zadkine.paris.fr; closed Mon*)

Musée Nissim de Camondo, for a mini Versailles in the centre of Paris, built by a wealthy Jewish banker who tragically died in battle in World War I. The rest of his family didn't survive the Holocaust and their orphaned house stands as a memory to them and other Jewish families lost in World War II.

(*63 rue Monceau, 8ème; lesartsdecoratifs.fr/en/museums/musee-nissim-de-camondo; closed Mon & Tues*)

Musée Bourdelle, for Antoine Bourdelle's secret garden of sculptures to rival Rodin's.

(*16-18 rue Antoine Bourdelle, 15ème; bourdelle.paris.fr; closed Mon*)

Unexpected Art Galleries

Cézanne and Renoir's Secret Artist Utopia

One could live in Paris their entire life and never discover the exquisite beauty of the **Villa des Arts**. Well hidden behind the chaotic hustle of *avenue de Clichy*, everything all of a sudden becomes so very peaceful and picturesque upon entering this little pocket of the 18th arrondissement, owed to the artistic community that has been discreetly cultivated here since the mid-1800s.

Villa des Arts

Paul Cézanne and his friend Auguste Renoir were once neighbours in this artist residence of light-filled ateliers set around a tranquil courtyard, ripe for painting. Picasso, Joan Miró, Gertrude Stein and André Breton were all regular visitors too, and later Fellini was seduced by the cinematic setting for his film *Les Clowns*. The *pièce de résistance* is the extraordinary double staircase inside the building marked by an old sign with 'Entrée des Artistes' on the door. Allegedly, the villa's architect used recycled materials from the Universal Exhibition of 1899 to patch it together.

To call this magnificent residence their home, working artists must apply to rent one of the studios via the Ville de Paris, which can be a lengthy and complicated process but is designed to ensure that the villa stays true to its vocation. For more than 200 years the residence has remained dedicated to housing creatives of all kinds, from painters to poets, and now part of the building is also let out as social housing.

While the gates of the Villa des Arts are not generally open to the public, residents will usually let you wander in after them for a peek inside; for a more official drop in, you can sign up for the guided visits on the first Sunday of every month. The lovely Brigitte can show you all the secrets of this little-known architectural treasure (in English, upon request) and you can also organise a special rendezvous with one of the artists-in-residence, who will show you around their studio.

(15 rue Hégésippe-Moreau, 18ème; villadesarts.paris; €7 per person for the open visits on the first Sunday of the month at 4pm and €10 per person for private visits with a minimum group size of ten people. For reservations, email: hautefeuille.brigitte@gmail. com. For the studio visit with Nicolas Schöffer in his atelier, email Éléonore Schöffer at eleonoredelavandeyra@gmail.com or call +33 1 47 42 73 26)

Pretend to be Antique Dealers for the day

The **Hôtel Drouot** is the world's oldest public auction house, which might sound intimidating, but you and I are just as welcome through the doors of this madhouse as any fine art or antique collectors. We can jump from one auction to another, moving from room to room, all of them resembling small theatres of merchantry. The action is non-stop, all day, simultaneously over two floors. It's common to find the entire contents of a Parisian household on the auction block, from the kitchenware to prized family paintings. There's something for all budgets and you might just see something you'd be willing to fight for.

(9 rue Drouot, 9ème; auction details at drouot.com; Mon-Sat)

Ghost Signs of Notre Dame

Paris is one giant outdoor art gallery if you keep your eyes peeled and remember to *look up*. Ghost signs and street art can be found across the city, but my favourites are on a charming little square by the riverbanks in the shadow of Notre Dame. Make plans for breakfast at **Les Gourmands**

Miniature model
of Café de Flore

de Notre Dame, which you'll find located directly underneath the most beautiful and well-preserved ghost sign in Paris. The rare frescoes cover the entire second floor of the building, advertising a bygone sign-painting company. Bonus points: find the window with the art nouveau advert for 'Sorbet Montebello' on the same square.
(*1 rue des Grands Degrés, 5ème; gourmands-de-notredame.fr; usually open from 7.30am*)

The Miniature Café Flore within Café Flore

It's more than just a café, it's a Parisian institution. Tourists and long-time bohemian residents alike cram together on the terrace to watch Paris go by. And yet many of them will have probably missed one of the eatery's most interesting little features: the 1/7th full-scale miniature model of Café de Flore within the Café de Flore.

Take your hot chocolate inside on a cold winter's day and amidst the art deco interior, unchanged since World War II, you might notice a peculiar box in the corner of the room, by the staircase. Go take a closer look. It is the work of Charles Matton, a celebrated French artist, writer and a long-time patron of Café de Flore. Matton wrote about his cherished Left Bank haunt, where he so often went to drink his Guignolet Kirsch and cross paths with Juliette Gréco or Jean-Paul Sartre, and when he died in 2008, Café de Flore placed a sheer black cloth over his work in mourning. The box is a permanent fixture at this Parisian brasserie, which has a rich heritage of exhibiting and promoting the arts.
(*172 boulevard Saint-Germain, 6ème; cafedeflore.fr; open every day, 7.30am-1.30am*)

A Private Pompidou

If you're looking to see some contemporary art, but big museums like the Centre Pompidou just don't do it for you, I think I know the perfect place. **VNH Gallery** is tucked away in a charming courtyard of the Marais; intimate and quiet enough to be one-on-one with the art, but big and bright enough to do justice to some really large-scale museum-worthy installations.
(*108 rue Vieille du Temple, 3ème; vnhgallery.com; Tues-Sat*)

Atelier Window Shopping

There are four floors of incredible handmade ceramics and objets d'art in a renovated old atelier of the Marais. These are pieces that should probably be kept in glass cases, but instead, you can touch, smell, hold and take home every last item in this unusual concept store. **Empreintes** also has a coffee shop and library; a light-filled meeting place for collectors and patrons of the arts.
(*5 rue de Picardie, 3ème; empreintes-paris.com; Mon-Sat, 11am-7pm*)

Coffee in a Historic Engraver's Studio

Marvel at the leather-embossed painted wall coverings, the intricate engravings everywhere you look, glassware to die for, and surreal taxidermy curated by Philippe Starck, while drinking superb Italian coffee inside this historic French monument. **Caffè Stern** was opened as a letterpress studio in 1834 by Moïse Stern, and hanging above the entrance inside the covered *Passage des Panoramas*, you can still see his old sign, marked with the years he was awarded a gold medal at the World's Fair. Stop in for a morning coffee, an afternoon glass of champagne, or splurge on a fancy Italian feast. There's so much to look at you might just be there all day.
(*47 Passage des Panoramas, 2ème; +33 1 75 43 63 10; Tues-Sat, 8.30am to midnight*)

My Cultural Calendar

Backstage Paris

For one weekend every September, the most secretive spaces in Paris (and across France) have an open door policy known as **Journée Patrimoine**. From the underground's ghost métro stations to the presidential greenhouse, the city is left unlocked for forty-eight hours. If you're on Instagram, use the account **@jepofficial** to get a sneak peek of places that arouse your curiosity. The most unusual locations might require reserving a place.
(*journeesdupatrimoine.culturecommunication.gouv.fr*)

Dancing in the Street

Every year on the eve of the summer solstice, Paris turns into a city of music to rival New Orleans on Mardi Gras. **Fête de la Musique** sees undiscovered artists take to the sidewalks, cafés and bars to host free ad hoc concerts. Singers will even serenade us from their apartment balconies. You can catch a blues concert on the corner, a pop-up opera a few doors down and then follow an African drumming troupe along the boulevard. The music doesn't stop until 7am. I like to catch the action in the smaller backstreets of the Haut Marais around *Le Carreau du Temple*.
(*3ème; Métro: Temple*)

Artist Atelier Open Days

In the private courtyards hiding behind the façades of the 20th arrondissement, there are scores of artists' workshops, many of which open their doors to the public for one weekend in September and one in May. It's a perfect excuse to nose around secret gardens, meet artists and inspect the artwork.
(*For maps and info, click on the '**Portes Ouvertes**' links for the Belleville neighbourhood in May: ateliers-artistes-belleville.fr; and Menilmontant in September: ateliersdemenilmontant.org*)

The Montmartre Wine Harvest

Paris still has working vineyards (I count eight) and the most famous one, the *Clos de Montmartre*, likes to throw a big street party for their annual harvest in October, known as the **Fête des Vendanges**. Since 1934, it's been a tradition for the local wine and gastronomy societies of Montmartre to host a festival of fireworks, street food, wine tastings, marching bands and folklore performances. It's also a rare opportunity to go behind the fence and walk amongst the grapes, and even taste the wine made by the vineyard, which produces around 1,500 half-litre bottles each year.
(*Reserve your visit to the vineyard at fetedesvendangesdemontmartre.com or call +33 1 40 03 94 70*)

Festival of Secret Gardens

During the last weekend of September, before autumn turns the leaves, the **Fête des Jardins** sees all the private gardens of Paris unlocked for the day. Gather fresh herbs with the sisters in their convent's secret garden at *Couvent des Soeurs d'Adoration* (5ème), or attend a wine tasting in the less well-known vineyards of the 19th and 20th arrondissements, in Belleville or at la Butte Bergeyre (pg. 125).

Weekend Thrifting

On any given weekend there are always local **brocantes** (nomadic antiques markets) pitching their tents somewhere in Paris; it's just a matter of finding out where. In early June, there's a particularly spectacular brocante that sets up shop around the fountain of *Place Saint-Sulpice*.
(*Check the brocantes calendar on vide-greniers.org/75-Paris*)

Vive le Vintage

Once or twice a year, the **Salon du Vintage** invites the best vintage dealers in Europe to come together under one glass roof at a beautifully restored nineteenth-century clothes market. Dive into a world of expertly curated kitsch, '60s furniture design, rare fashion finds and retro entertainment.
(*See the salonduvintage.com for upcoming dates*)

Foodie Feasts

To get a taste of Paris's most promising food talent, look out for **Le Food Market**, a pop-up that hosts evening street feasts in the city's most vibrant neighbourhoods. Talented chefs from the hottest restaurants bring their kitchens to the boulevard and rustle up their most talked-about dishes to sample on picnic tables under string lights.
(*Find their next event on facebook.com/lefoodmarketparis or lefoodmarket.fr*)

The Real Summer Festival

Macki Music Festival in July is one of the summer music events really worth putting in your calendar, especially if undiscovered bands and bohemian vibes are your bag.
(*mackimusicfestival.fr*)

Couvent des Soeurs (Courtesy of L'instant Parisien/linstantparisien.com)

04

Lonely Hearts Club

Dear Nessy,

I don't know why I feel like I can tell you this, but I just got my heart broken. I know we don't know each other personally but reading your blog almost every day makes me feel in some way that we do. In a bid to escape, I've booked a ticket to Paris, maybe in the hopes that I'll be able to heal myself there. It may seem like a strange choice after a break-up, since Paris is one of the most romantic destinations in the world, but your city has always called out to me. With romance the furthest thing from my mind, do you have any recommendations for a wounded heart? Aside from drowning my sorrows in bottles of French wine (although I'm not totally opposed to that idea either), is there a side to Paris that might help me come to terms with being alone again?

Thank you,
From a friend you've never met

You're not alone. As much as I don't like to admit it to myself, I guess I came to Paris with a broken heart too, or at least a disillusioned one. Your urge to flee to Paris, one of the most romantic cities in the world, isn't strange at all. If anything, take it as a sign that you haven't quite given up on the idea of love. I'm not promising that you'll find all the answers strolling the banks of the Seine, but I can promise you that Paris is actually one of the best cities to go it alone. Here, solitude is made even more appealing. There's a funny sort of romance to it. This is your chance to celebrate and enjoy life's small pleasures again without the distraction of someone who may have kept you from noticing them. Sit in a café and observe the eccentric characters; imagine their stories, what makes them laugh and what makes them cry, who they've loved and who they've lost. At the markets, secretly plunge your hand into a bag of grains while no one is looking and try all the melty cheese from the fromagerie because you can. Write letters to a stranger while swinging your legs over the edge of the Canal Saint-Martin with a bottle of wine. Be in a world of your own. That's just what Paris is for.

How to Lose the Paris Blues

Sing Along to 'La Vie en Rose'

Chez Louisette is a kitschy little bistro that's been around since 1967, hidden deep in the oldest part of the Paris flea market. Hungry antique hunters and dealers alike squeeze around long tables for a hearty lunch and the good-time ambience of old-timey singers belting out numbers by Piaf and other favourites. Accompanied by a nostalgic accordion, you might even end up dancing on the tables come dessert.

(Enter Marché Vernaison at 99 rue des Rosiers and find it down the rabbit hole; 93400 Saint-Ouen; +33 1 40 12 10 14)

Paris in a Sidecar

Feel the wind in your hair, racing down the Parisian boulevards and whizzing through backstreets, escorted by a time-travelling gentleman 'sidecarist'. Climb aboard the classic bikes of **Retro Tours** and choose your own tailor-made route, or discover their 'Great Escapes' and night rides. I don't usually recommend organised tours, but this one guarantees smiles from ear to ear.

(Takes 1-2 passengers, more info on retro-tour.com/en)

Chez Louisette

Here's looking at you, kid

The Latin Quarter is home to several independent picture houses from the 1970s specialising in old American cinema. I go for the joy of buying tickets from those old-fashioned ticket booths and the soothing innocence of technicolour movies. See what's playing at **Cinema Christine 21** (*4 rue Christine, 6ème; christine21.cine.allocine.fr*) and **Le Desperado** (*23 rue des Ecoles, 5ème; desperado. cine.allocine.fr*)

Right: Rue Cremieux

Opposite: Le Refuge des Fondues

My Little Portobello in Paris

Speaking of technicolour, I recommend seeking out the ***rue Cremieux*** for a whimsical stroll down the most cheerful street in Paris, lined with a rainbow of colourful chocolate-box houses. The residents went the extra mile on their façades with the addition of trompe l'oeil paintwork, so that each house tells its own story.
(*Rue Cremieux, 12ème*)

Fondue Folly

Leave your grown-up pants at the door of **Le Refuge des Fondues** and prepare for the silliest dining experience, which involves drinking wine from a baby bottle and feasting on fondue inside a cosy carnivalesque den in Montmartre. Why the wine in the baby bottles? It's no gimmick; it's the owners trick to avoid the French tax on wine glasses. Rub elbows on long communal tables with a mix of Parisians and fellow travellers who don't take themselves too seriously. Try the meat fondue in a savoury broth if you're all cheesed out.
(*17 rue des Trois Frères, 18ème; open every day for dinner until 2am, reservations on +33 1 42 55 22 65*)

Sunday Smiles

To beat the end-of-week blues, head on over for an evening at **Le Cinquante**, a genuine *bar du quartier*. The food and drinks are very affordable, the decor is nostalgic and the locals get kinda crazy close to midnight, especially on Sunday's open-mic night. There's a piano in one of the dining rooms at the back, which makes for a jovial birthday gathering.
(*50 rue de Lancry, 10ème; +33 1 42 02 36 83; open every day, 6pm-2am*)

Old-School Arcade Lovers

You're sure to find some of the most eccentric locals of Montmartre hanging at **La Divette de Montmartre**, a 1960s-style bar and tabac filled with arcade games and *le babyfoot* – French for foosball.
(*136 rue Marcadet, 18ème; +33 1 46 06 19 64; Mon-Sat, 5pm-1am*)

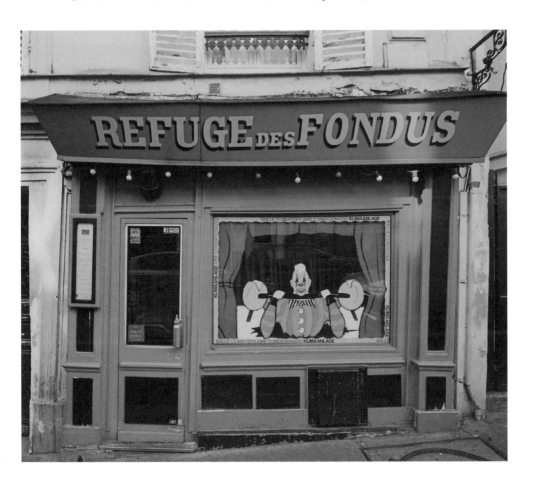

Where to strike up conversations (or best overhear them)

With theatrical locals at the oldest bar in Paris

When **Le Bar de l'Entracte** first opened in 1614, it catered to late-night carriage drivers stopping by for a beer and bathroom break on their way home from dropping courtesans at the royal palace next door. When the theatre across the street opened in 1790, it became the after-show refuge of actors and performers. Expect some theatrics from the café owner, but don't worry, he's harmless – even after a few glasses behind the bar. Take a seat at the cosy corner terrace (heated in winter), order some wine and a plate of charcuterie (or whatever the owner has in his fridge), sit back and watch the show unfold.
(*47 rue de Montpensier, 1er; +33 1 80 97 40 00; Mon-Sat, 10am-1am, Sunday, 12pm-8pm*)

Le Bar de l'Entracte

Book parties of the boho-intello-chic

I like to think of the brother and sister team behind Ofr as a little bit like today's answer to Sylvia Beach, the famed patron and publisher of James Joyce and Hemingway, whose English bookshop (Shakespeare & Co.) became the cultural axis for the entire Left Bank. Except Ofr, short for 'open, free and ready', sits across the river on the Right Bank and has an unmistakable Parisian flair about it. Under the tastemaking curation of Alexandre and Marie Thumerelle,

this contemporary bookstore, gallery and library of rare indie magazines has served as the cultural axis for the boho-intello-chic generation living in Paris over the last two decades. Filled with an eclectic selection of both English and French print, some of it published in-house, Ofr hosts frequent social events, at least two a week, from book releases and mini art exhibits to live concerts. And they're all open, free and ready for your visit.
(*20 Rue Dupetit-Thouars, 3ème; Mon-Sat, 10am-8pm, Sun, 2pm-7pm*)

My Tiki Bar
Lone Palm is the kind of place you'd imagine finding Hunter S. Thompson sitting at the booth in the corner. Cocktails have names like the 'Salton Sea' and 'Canyon Drive', and the friendly barman keeps the conversation in this tiny bar flowing.
(*21 rue Keller, 11ème; lonepalm.fr; open every day, 6pm-2am*)

A local sense of humour test
Parisians aren't exactly known for being warm and fuzzy, but they do like to tease occasionally and warm to you when you show you have a sense of humour or a little sass. A meal at **Au Bistro** is a sociable experience, where a bit of playful banter (even in English) goes a long way with the after-work crowd of locals – a.k.a. the cheeky boss and his goodtime band of buddies. The 'Mrs' is also there to keep an eye on the boys from behind the bar. An authentic family-run joint situated unexpectedly in the heart of the posh luxury-shopping paradise of the 1er arrondissement, Au Bistro offers an out-of-time Parisian experience and an opportunity to try excellent authentic French food. Score extra points with the locals if you order the Andouillette sausage.
(*8 rue du Marché Saint-Honoré, 1er; +33 1 42 61 02 45; open for breakfast, lunch & dinner Mon- Fri, and on Sat, 8am-4pm*)

Ex-pat Apéro
A crowd of trendy ex-pats gather at the deceivingly divey **Martin** to unwind on natural wines and deliciously adventurous finger foods, such as jalapeño razor clams and duck heart teriyaki skewers.
(*24 boulevard du temple, 11ème; +33 1 43 57 82 37; bar-martin.fr; closed Sun & Mon*)

Making friends with your elbows
The tables at **Le Cherche Midi** are set in such a way that it's impossible to leave without having made new friends. It usually starts with your immediate neighbour recommending their favourite dish and ends with you sharing each other's desserts. This friendly family-style restaurant, converted from an old hotel lobby, is arguably the best Italian food in Paris.
(*22 rue du Cherche-Midi, 6ème;lecherchemidi.fr; open daily for lunch & dinner*)

The place you wish you lived upstairs from

A wine bar and eatery housed in a tiny 1930s cheese shop with the old tiles, mosaic floor and zinc counter still intact, **La Buvette** has a way of making you feel totally at ease despite a lack of space. Whether you're conscientious, curious or just totally confused about the natural (organic) wine movement, the young owner Camille is probably the least pretentious sommelier in Paris to talk with about it. Getting her advice on an inexpensive glass from her obscure wine collection to help get you started is part of the experience. She serves simple but delicious sharing plates from €3-€12, on what I suspect is her grandmother's china.

(67 rue Saint-Maur, 11ème; +33 9 83 56 94 11; open Wed & Thurs, 5pm-10pm; Fri-Sun, 11am-10pm)

*Also see the 'Wine bar in a Bookshop' on pg. 35.

Feeding a Broken Heart (or a Hangover)

Whether you're hankering for the comfort of a perfect steak frites, the most drool-worthy dessert, or you're just in need of something ... well, not so French – here's how to treat yourself to a well-deserved feast at the foodie haunts that call my name on an empty stomach. I can't guarantee they'll cure a broken heart, but they'll certainly help a hangover, which may or may not have been my disposition while compiling this shortlist.

The giant soufflé at **Le Bon George**: call to request this secret menu item in advance, it's that important.
(45 rue Saint-Georges, 9ème; +33 1 48 78 40 30; open Mon-Fri for lunch & dinner)

The giant mozzarella platters at **Pizza Popolare**: one of several restaurants of the successful Big Mama group, kings of affordable Italian cuisine in Paris, you can get a Margherita pizza here for €5. No reservations.
(111 rue Réaumur, 2ème; +33 1 42 21 30 91; open every day for lunch & dinner)

Pot-au-feu chicken in baguette sandwiches at **Chez Aline**: gourmet French food to go or to eat in at the tiny bar inside a former horse butchers.
(85 rue de la Roquette, 11ème; +33 1 43 71 90 75; open Mon-Fri, 11am- 5.30pm)

French food porn on *rue des Martyrs*: think of it like a farmers' market, except all these farmers upgraded to brick-and-mortar boutiques located conveniently on one street at the foot of Montmartre. (9ème)

Les Bols de Jean

Chocolate baguette bread from the **Liberté** boulangerie: a specialist bakery worth stopping at on your way to a picnic on the canal.
(*39 rue des Vinaigriers, 10ème; libertepatisserieboulangerie.com; open breakfast-8pm*)

Taste-bud tingling tapas plates at **Ellsworth** and *that dessert*: chocolate sherbet, malt ice cream with salty crumble, espresso foam and meringue. Grab an early seat at the marble bar or reserve ahead.
(*34 rue de Richelieu, 1er; book online at ellsworthparis.com; open Tues-Sat for lunch & dinner, Sun for brunch, Mon for dinner*)

Adorable bread bowls at **Les Bols de Jean**: from Mushroom risotto topped with a poached egg to a cheesy shepherd's pie, your food is served inside a toasted and buttered brioche, so you can scoop out the insides and devour your dish until there is nothing left. The most unique lunch in the city – eat in or takeaway.
(*2 rue de Choiseul, 2ème; bolsdejean.com; open Mon-Sat, 10am-4pm, and Thurs for dinner*)

Instagrammable cheat days at **Broken Biscuits**: different from standard patisserie fare, make this beautiful little café your reward at the end of a Sunday stroll.
(*10 Passage Rochebrune, 11ème; open Wed-Sun*)

Le Bon Georges

The Pekinese dumplings (*raviolis pékinois*) on Thursday and Sunday at **Au Pays de Sourire**: this is a most welcoming and kitschy old Chinese restaurant where you can eat like a king for the price of a pauper. Also sample the *porc en lamelle* that comes served with pancakes and plum sauce.
(*32 rue de Bièvre, 5ème; +33 1 43 26 15 69; closed Sun*)

The truffle croque monsieur and melt-in-your-mouth burrata at **Le Distrait**: a sleek and trendy dinner spot hidden behind the grands boulevards.
(*26 rue de la Lune, 2ème; reserve at ledistrait.fr; Tues-Sat, 6.30pm-2am*)

The Chinese 'spaghetti bolognese' at **Trois Fois Plus Piment**: when they ask what level of spiciness you want on your Sichuan beef noodles, from 1 to 10, say 1 – trust me, it's spicy enough.
(*184 rue Saint-Martin, 3ème; +33 6 52 66 75 31; open Tues-Sun for lunch & dinner*)

The salad menu at **Le Comptoir**: I would even recommend ordering one as a starter and one as a main.
(*5 Carrefour de l'Odéon, 6ème; +33 1 43 29 12 05; open every day for lunch & dinner, but go on weekends when there's no set menu and no reservations*)

The steak frites at **Le Bistrot Paul Bert**: leave the tourists to queue up at the famous and overrated Entrecôte chain while you try the real deal. If only you could drink that sauce from a glass.
(*18 rue Paul Bert, 11ème; +33 1 43 72 24 01; open Tues-Sat for lunch & dinner*)

Pastrami sandwiches at **Schwartz** for homesick New Yorkers: a Sunday institution in Paris's vibrant Jewish community.
(*16 rue des Ecouffes, 4ème; +33 2 78 84 99 99; open every day for lunch & dinner*)

The fish and chips at **The Sunken Chip** for Brits missing home: a stylish sanctuary for the salt and vinegar inclined.
(*39 rue des Vinaigriers, 10ème; thesunkenchip.com; open Tues-Sun for lunch & dinner*)

A nocturnal Caribbean feast at **Babylone Bis**: discover some seriously delicious chicken dishes with banana plantain and coconut rice to soak up a long night of partying. This kitschy twenty-something-year-old Antillese kitchen has fed the likes of everyone from Marvin Gaye to Rihanna. Open officially from 8pm to 5am, open unofficially until 7am.
(*34 rue Tiquetonne, 2ème; +33 1 42 33 48 35; Wed-Sun*)

Burger addicts: help settle the Parisian burger war between **Le Camion Qui Fume** (*168 rue Montmartre, 2ème; lecamionquifume.com*) and **Blend** (*44 rue d'Argout, 2ème; blendhamburger.com*). Which one deserves the title for best burger in Paris? Both open for lunch and dinner.

All-you-can-eat DIY Chinese fondue at **Au Ciel**: order the '*Menu à Volonté*' – choose between five different flavoured broths for dipping and use the order form to mark off the unlimited list of ingredients you want cooked in front of you.
(*19 bd Saint-Martin, 3ème; auciel.fr; open all day every day except Wed; dinner only*)

Brilliant breakfast buffet for a bargain at **Mama Shelter**: they have giant sofas to park yourself on for the morning with your laptop. €16 a head.
(*109 rue de Bagnolet, 20ème; mamashelter.com; buffet until 11am Mon-Sat, restaurant open all day*)

Top 5 for Detox Day
(after too much wine and cheese)

1   **Greenhouse**: Organic vegetable and healthy bowl hangout with California roots and natural wine. Always expect a warm welcome from the American owner, Kristin Frederick.
    (*22 rue Crespin du Gast, 11ème; open lunch & dinner, closed Sun & Mon*)

2   **Nanashi**: Healthy Parisian-Japanese bento.
    (*31 rue de Paradis, 10ème; nanashi.fr; open every day for lunch & dinner; Sun, lunch only*)

3   **Café Pinson**: Wheat-free, dairy-free superfood.
    (*6 rue du Forez, 3ème; cafepinson.fr; open every day for lunch & dinner; Sun, lunch only*)

4   **Wild & the Moon**: The city's hippest juice bar.
    (*55 rue Charlot, 3ème; wildandthemoon.com; open every day, 8am-7pm*)

5   **Season**: Ladies lunching over quinoa and tuna tataki.
    (*1 rue Charles-François Dupuis, 3ème; season-paris.com; open every day for lunch & dinner, Sun, lunch only*)

Greenhouse
(photo courtesy
Edouard Grandjea

All Dressed Up & Nowhere to Go?

Clandestine Cocktails

On a leafy avenue in Montmartre, inside the former villa of the Hermès family, at the top of a secret stairway, the Hôtel Particulier de Montmartre has a very special bar called **Le Très Particulier**. Spoil yourself with luxurious cocktails and schmooze with a diverse crowd of well-travelled guests of the hotel and in-the-know Parisians that come for the weekend DJ.
(*Enter through the gate at 23 avenue Junot, 18ème; +33 1 53 41 81 40; open every day till 2am*)

I imagine **Maison Souquet** as the perfect place for an international spy to wind down in his tuxedo after a long day. This former Belle Époque brothel is now a beautifully restored boutique hotel and lounge, with antique velvet conversation chairs, expert mood lighting and a whole lot of sophisticated sex appeal.
(*10 rue de Bruxelles, 9ème; maisonsouquet.com; +33 1 48 78 55 55; open every day till 2am*)

Behind an unmarked wooden door in the Left Bank, the **Castor Club** is a warm and welcoming den whether you're dressed to the nines or just wandering by in your jeans and t-shirt. Their cocktails set the standard in Paris, the bartenders couldn't be friendlier and there's also a unique selection of rare scotches at fair prices. Blues music is on the ground floor and a DJ plays '50s/'60s/'70s music downstairs in the eighteenth-century wine cellar.
(*14 rue de Hautefeille, 6ème; +33 9 50 64 99 38; open Tues-Sat, 7pm till late.*)

Since you're nearby, I'd also hop over to the **Prescription**, the rival cocktail bar down the road where the ambience is a little less casual and more suited to a flirtatious meeting of strangers in the night.
(*23 rue Mazarine, 6ème; +33 9 50 35 72 87; open every day, 7pm till late*)

The Beef Club Ballroom, a lavish basement bar at the bottom of a spiral staircase, gets very lively with the single Parisian crowd on the prowl. The music is swinging, the drinks catch on fire and by closing time at 2am, you'll emerge buzzing from this underground ball.
(*58 rue Jean-Jacques Rousseau, 1er, +33 9 54 37 13 65; eccbeefclub.com; open every day, 8pm till late*)

Havana Nights in Paris

In the setting of an old biscuit factory, at **Studio de l'Ermitage** you will meet Paris's Latino community, dance your pants off around a live band and feel like

you're in South America for the night. It's best known for the Latin American nights and buying tickets online is advisable as these events really do sell out. Ladies, wear comfortable shoes and bring a fan if you have one.
(*8 rue de l'Ermitage, 20ème; +33 1 55 78 84 75; see the website for details: studio-ermitage.com*)

If you haven't planned ahead but already have your dancing shoes on, try the **Barrio Latino**, best described as something between a New Orleans saloon bar and a Cuban dancehall. Every night, in this nineteenth-century space built by Gustave Eiffel, there are informal sessions for Cuban salsa, swing, tango and samba.
(*46-48 rue du Faubourg Saint-Antoine, 12ème; barrio-latino.com; open every day, 12pm-3am*)

*Also see 'Tango on the Seine' pg. 57, and find more nightlife tips in the next chapter...

Right: Studio de l'Ermitage

Le Dépanneur Terrasse

05

Don't Call me a Hipster, but...

Hey Ness,

I don't really like labels, but I guess I like a lot of the things they call 'hipster' these days. Yes, I'm drawn to bars that have old-world lightbulbs, beautiful typography on the menu and staff that wear retro graphic t-shirts instead of tailcoats. I enjoy being around the aesthetically inclined and the entrepreneurial types who seem to own their town. So my question is (hopefully without sounding too pretentious): where do the 'cool kids' hang out in Paris; where do they really shop, eat, drink and go out?

Magdalena
Sent from my iPhone

Ah yes, the hipster's don't-call-me-a-hipster dilemma. Every generation has had its own buzzword for those who seem to define what's 'cool' – artistic and bohemian in some form, keenly in tune with the way things look, taste, sound, feel and smell. In the seventies it was the hippies, in the sixties the mods, the beatniks in the fifties and long before that it was the libertines. I don't think we need to be too squeamish about the word 'hipster'. Let's just agree it has something to do with the gilded youth looking for an escape from what's considered normal. Of course, not even Paris can say it's steered clear of hipster overkill (cafés, bars and shops that look identically 'quirky'). It's worth doing a bit of homework to find out about the urban creatives who are really pushing the envelope with original concepts and taking note of the neighbourhoods that most welcome this kind of innovation. But I'll let you copy my homework.

Social Playgrounds in the Sun

Sunset Spritzers behind the Windmill of the Moulin Rouge
Once used as a backstage area for the Moulin Rouge, find the hidden rooftop
terrace **Bar à Bulles**, tucked away behind the iconic red windmill, where
the can-can girls of yesteryear would sunbathe in the nude and rehearse
their routines in the summer months. One rooftop over lived Boris Vian, the
bohemian 'prince' of Paris and leading promoter of American jazz music, who
pioneered a movement that brought back the city's *joie de vivre* following the
war.

Stay for dinner under the fairy lights or come for the brunch at the weekend.
You can catch an exhibition, pop-up market or even a live rooftop gig during
the warmer season.
(*4 Cité Véron, 18ème; +33 9 73 23 79 72; Wed-Fri, 6pm till late; Sat, 12pm till late; Sun,
12pm till 7pm. For events check facebook.com/barabulleslamachine*)

Bar à Bulles

41

A Moveable Makeshift Feast

In recent years, an anti-establishment collective calling themselves **Ground Control** has been transforming giant forgotten urban spaces into ephemeral summer playgrounds. Here, one can play pétanque on old railway tracks next to a flourishing veggie garden, attend concerts in abandoned warehouses, sip wine whilst thrift shopping, or sample the best of the Parisian food-truck scene before playing a game of ping-pong under fairy lights next to a chicken coop. The free-spirited informal scene emerges in April/May and lasts through to October, usually open from Wednesday to Sunday from lunchtime until late. The ephemeral collective tends to change its location every few seasons, but a quick Facebook search of 'Ground Control' or the official website should bring you up to date on this year's location and events programme.
(*facebook.com/GroundControlParis or Groundcontrolparis.com*)

The Industrial Treehouse

The year-round rooftop terrace of **Le Perchoir** is always ready and waiting, with heated tent areas, summer vibes (even in winter) and a great view over the city. Located on the seventh floor of an old unmarked industrial building, this popular bar may require some waiting time downstairs if you don't arrive early enough (unless you've booked dinner in the restaurant on the sixth floor). Keep an eye on the Facebook page for art and fashion events or foodie pop-ups.
(*14 rue Crespin du Gast, 11ème; +33 1 48 06 18 48; open every day, 4pm-2am; facebook. com/leperchoir.restaurant*)

Glamping in the City

For quality time with the birds and the bees, the Parisian *jeunesse* will rendezvous at the Parc de Buttes Chaumont in the 19th arrondissement, hosting picnics on the grass or meeting at the park's dreamy **Pavillon Puebla**, a restored belvedere from the Belle Époque. In the winter it can take on the personality of a 1920s cabaret hidden in the forest, and come summer, it morphs into a Navajo-inspired glamping experience. More of a destination for the drinks than the food, lively entertainment and DJ sets are usually on the menu too.
(*Parc des Buttes Chaumont, avenue Darcel, 19ème; +33 1 42 39 34 20; open Wed-Fri, 6pm-1.45am; Sat, noon-1.45am; Sun, noon-9pm; facebook.com/Pavillonpuebla/*)

Floating Plunge Pool on the Seine

The first floating hotel in France, **OFF Paris Seine** boasts fifty-eight contemporary rooms and a very tempting plunge pool running the length of the restaurant and bar. Hotel guests of the purpose-built barge have private access to the pool for most of the day, but from 5pm until 1am, we're invited for poolside cocktails with the resident golden swan, Marcel (a name I bestowed upon the hotel's floating blow-up duck).
(*20-22 Port d'Austerlitz, 13ème; +33 1 44 06 62 65; offparisseine.com*)

Left: OFF Paris Seine
Opposite: Ground Control

Shopping like a Parisian

Canal Saint-Martin

Better known for its quaint waterside views and apéro spots than for shopping, it's easy to miss out on some very interesting retail therapy in Canal Saint-Martin. So here's the key to the quartier: *rue de Marseille* and *rue Beaurepaire* – as long as you have these two neighbouring streets on your radar, you'll be on the right track. Wander in and out of converted old Parisian ateliers with a Williamsburg NYC retail vibe, discovering hip young brands and concept boutiques, especially for the guys. You can also find a few end-of-season outlets for Sandro, Maje and Claudie Pierlot.
(*10ème; Métro: Jacques Bonsergent; most shops open Mon-Sat & Sun afternoon*)

Boutiques not to miss: Centre Commercial, Agnès B, Nordkraft, Atelier Green Factory, A.P.C., Antoine et Lili
Break for a bite: The Sunken Chip, Siseng, Jules et Shim, Le Verre Volé, Hôtel du Nord
Coffee shops: Ten Belles, Café Craft, Le Comptoir Générale

Rue de Charonne

Hidden away behind bustling Bastille, at the beginning of *rue de Charonne* a new shopping village of independent fashion boutiques has quietly emerged in the last five years. While *rue de Charonne* is tailor-made for an afternoon of shopping with the girls, the boys have staked their claim here too, with boutiques selling sturdy leathers and sartorial gear. Even little ones will find some artisanal toy shops and the latest trends in micro fashion – hence the family ambience that spills out onto the café terraces on sunny Saturdays.
(*11ème; Métro: Ledru Rollin; most shops open Tues-Sat*)

Boutiques not to miss: La Fée Maraboutée, So We Are, Sessùn, Les Fleurs (around the corner on *rue Trusseau*)
Break for a bite: Pause Café, Le Souk (*1 rue Keller*), Clamato

Etienne Marcel & le Sentier

Start with the cobblestoned *rue Tiquetonne* for its vintage havens and skater-boy concept stores that always make me think of this street as a 'Little California'. Here you'll find **Kiliwatch**, the capital's destination vintage store; a jungle of colourful Liberty-print dresses, Levi's 501s, well-loved leather, Barbour jackets, and those Breton striped shirts of which every Parisian keeps at least five variations in their closet at all times. Around the corner on *rue Montmartre* pop into the **Yaya Store** for the style aesthetic of a Parisian bohemian explorer, and accessorise with high-street classics at & Other Stories and Cos. Next, take

the *rue Montorgeuil*, one of the oldest market streets in Paris, and continue walking north where it becomes the *rue des Petits Carreaux*, taking you through the Sentier, the city's historic garment district of wholesalers and former textile factories. If you get peckish, keep your eye out for **Boneshaker Donuts**, the friendliest, most creative donut shop this side of the Atlantic (*at the corner of rue des Petits Carreaux and rue d'Aboukir, 2ème; Tues-Sat, 10-6pm*). When the road name changes again into *rue des Poissonniere*, take a left onto *rue des Jeuneurs* until you reach the final destination on your shopping pilgrimage, the **Appartement Sézane** (*1 rue Saint-Fiacre, 2ème; Wed-Sat, 11am-8pm*). Think Anthropologie but better (and French). The bricks-and-mortar showroom of this online-only French cult clothing brand is like hanging out in a fashionista's dream apartment for an intimate masterclass in Parisian style. Touch and try the collections and they'll deliver to you within forty-eight hours.
(*2ème; Métro: Étienne Marcel; most shops open Mon-Sat*)

Boutiques not to miss: Yaya Store, Kiliwatch Vintage store, Episode Vintage, American Vintage, Appartement Sezane
Break for a bite: Blend on *rue d'Argout* or Balzac's old favourite, Au Rocher de Cancaleon (*rue Montorgeuil*)

Saint-Sulpice
Parisian boutique shopping at its most picturesque and plentiful can be found in the small streets behind *boulevard Saint-Germain*. Alternate French fashion favourites such as Agnès B and Hervé Chapellier with charming antique shops and interior design stores. From the Saint-Sulpice métro, follow the *rue du Vieux Colombier* until you reach the fountains in front of the famous Église Saint-Sulpice (the *Da Vinci Code* church). Then start doing a back-and-forth zigzag of the shopping streets that veer off the *rue Saint-Sulpice*, such as *rue Bonaparte*, *rue des Cannettes* (good for the boys), *rue Mabillon*, and finally *rue de Seine*.
(*6ème; Métro: Saint-Sulpice; most shops open every day*)

Boutiques not to miss: Les 3 Marchés de Catherine B, Jinji, Hervé Chapellier, Agnès B, Souleiado
Break for a bite: Café de la Mairie, Le Machon d'Henri

Haut Marais
If you were to tell a Parisian taxi driver to take you to the Marais, they would more than likely just drop you off smack in the middle of the most crowded and touristy part of it. Don't get me wrong, you'll find shops there, but mostly commercial high street ones you've seen a thousand times before. You want the *real* Marais where the real Parisians shop – also known as the 'Haut Marais'. Use the *rue de Bretagne* as your axis to navigate the backstreets and discover

Empreintes boutique,
5 Rue de Picardie in the
Haut Marais

creative little boutiques selling up-and-coming labels and Parisian classics to complete that effortless low-key Parisian 'bobo' (bohemian bourgeois) look.

For a more down-to-earth version of the famous Colette boutique, stop in at the **Merci concept store** (*111 boulevard Beaumarchais, 3ème; Mon-Sat, 10-7pm*) and across the boulevard, shop for quirky basic tees and sweats at the trendy **Maison Kitsuné** (*18 boulevard des Filles du Calvaire, 11ème; open every day*). Once you think you've discovered it all, take the time to go down the *rue Vieille du Temple* and visit the old Jewish quarter in the classic Marais.
(*3ème; Métro: Filles du Calvaire or Temple; most shops open Tues-Sun*)

Boutiques not to miss: Merci Concept Store, The Broken Arm, Maison Kitsuné, Tom Greyhound Paris, Empreintes, Zou Boutique
Break for a bite: Café Charlot, Marché des Enfants Rouge, Candeleria, La Petite Table

Dining with the Cool Kids

Vintage Revival

If you want to meet the modern-day Jane Birkins of Paris, book yourself a table at **Aux Deux Amis** and find her lookalikes leaning over the Formica bar of this tiny old-school Parisian café, which looks like it's stuck somewhere in the sixties. You'll understand what lures the crowd here once you start sampling their very modern and minimalist twist on the freshest of Mediterranean ingredients. The menu is handwritten on the waiter's notepad; order around five plates between two people.
(*45 rue Oberkampf, 11ème; +33 1 58 30 38 13; Tues-Sat, 10.30am-2am*)

Next to an impressive 1852 circus arena right in the middle of Paris, the **Clown Bar** once catered to hungry lion tamers and acrobats of the Belle Époque, and has the tiling and frescoes to prove it. Today it's become a favourite destination of Michelin-star chefs on their days off, wowed by the edgy Japanese flair added to traditional French cuisine.
(*114 rue Amelot, 11ème; +33 1 43 55 87 35; open Wed-Sun*)

Hidden in back alley graffiti haven in Belleville, **Le Grand Bain** is a Michelin-star worthy restaurant disguised as and priced like a dive bar, not to be missed by any serious foodies. British chef Edward Delling Williams (previously of Au Passage restaurant) has an extreme focus on culinary innovation and quality of ingredients, and you can watch the whole show through a glass window separating kitchen and restaurant. Natural wines and adventurous sharing plates keep the place buzzing every night of the week and Edward's ex-pat crowd gathers for his British roast on Sundays.
(*14 rue Denoyez, 20 ème; +33 1 85 15 23 13; open every night for dinner and Sunday for lunch; online bookings: legrandbainparis.com*)

Fashion Week Secrets

Book a table at **Hôtel Providence** to feel like you're a guest in an eccentric Parisian townhouse, hosted by a worldly bohemian who enjoys late nights discussing anything taboo over oysters, smoked pork and the perfect Manhattan by the fire, surrounded by velvet everything. If you want to stretch the night further at this former nineteenth-century brothel, see if any of their rooms are available; equipped with custom-made cocktail bars, built-in ice-makers and turntables, the fashion week set is known to throw secret Nouvelle Vague after-parties here. Order lobster sandwiches and black truffles on toast to your room at any hour of the night.
(*90 rue René Boulanger, 10ème; +33 1 46 34 34 04; hotelprovidenceparis.com; open every day*)

Hôtel Providence

The nondescript façade of Chinese restaurant **Davé** could easily be mistaken for a questionable massage parlour, hiding behind clandestine red velvet curtains. You would never guess that it's actually one of the most legendary celebrity haunts in Paris, counting such icons as the late Yves Saint Laurent among its loyal patrons over the years, all thanks to the eccentric owner and head waiter, whose name is, of course, Dave. It's dimly lit like an opium den and the ghost of Yves Saint Laurent himself could indeed be reading his paper in the corner booth over a plate of dumplings, incognito. Covering the walls, Dave's collection of Polaroids, in which he's posing cheek to cheek with the world's most revered fashion, film and music icons, could fill an exhibition. During fashion week, this cult restaurant becomes a hush-hush celebrity haven between shows for the likes of Anna Wintour, Grace Coddington and Dave's supermodel friends. (*12 rue de Richelieu, 1er; +33 1 42 61 49 48*)

Cibus is another secret fashion week address – a tiny, very authentic Italian restaurant with only eight tables behind the preserved art nouveau façade of a former perfume boutique. Order the sea urchin pasta, a house speciality not always on the menu, reserved only for those who know to ask for it. (*5 rue Moliere, 1er; +33 1 42 61 50 19; closed Sun*)

Toast of the Town

In an up-and-coming residential area of Paris you wouldn't necessarily discover otherwise, there's an award-winning bistro called **Septime**, which, since it opened in 2011, has been consistently ranked among Paris's top ten restaurants. Refreshingly different to most Michelin-star restaurants, the look is inspired by an artisan's rustic workshop and the menu is an organic, modern take on French classics. Scoring a dinner reservation, however, is predictably tricky, so to avoid disappointment try a lunch seating – you'll get to enjoy the pretty back garden during the day, and at €30 it's half the price too. If you prefer spontaneity to making reservations, try the sister restaurant next door, **Clamato**, which specialises in seafood-related tapas. Get there at 7pm to grab my favourite spot for two at the bar, next to the window on the left as soon as you walk in. The menu changes all the time, depending on what type of oysters and seafood are in season. If they impress you with their food, try the **Septime Cave** (*3 rue Basfroi*), a wine bar across the road which is open Tuesday to Saturday, serving excellent house charcuterie complemented by an unusual vino menu ideal for an apéro.

(*80 rue de Charonne, 11ème; +33 1 43 67 38 29; septime-charonne.fr for opening times*)

A Feast for the Eyes

You'll be greeted by a stuffed flying wolf and a lynx wearing a diamond necklace at the entrance of **Caffè Stern**, a lavish cabinet of curiosities inside the covered *Passage des Panoramas*. This historic letterpress studio has been revived by designer Philippe Starck and an award-winning team of Italian chefs. The cuisine is gourmet Italian and the bill can run high, but you can find a €38 menu for lunch and coffee.

(*47 Passage des Panoramas, 2ème; +33 1 75 43 63 10; Tues-Sat, 8.30am to midnight*)

Mama Primi, **Ober Mama** and **East Mama** are three locations of a growing Italian food empire in Paris. They're also just about the only restaurants that Parisians are willing to queue for (they don't take reservations). Generous portions of only the best Italian products are served on the most charming hand-painted porcelain that will have you fighting the urge not to snap that bird's-eye Instagram of your meal. The cocktails are dangerously pretty too, and don't forget to order the all-you-can-eat Nutella jar served with pizza bread for dessert.

(*Primi: 71 rue des Dames, 17ème/Ober: 107 boulevard Richard Lenoir, 10ème/East: 133 rue du Faubourg Saint-Antoine, 11ème; bigmammagroup.com; all open Mon- Sun for lunch & dinner*)

Who gets the award for the most beautifully plated food in Paris? That would probably be **Dilia**, a small, intimate restaurant hidden away in the 20th

Hôtel Grand Amour

arrondissement, fixing for a Michelin star. The interior design might be simple but the food presentation is exquisite, and yes, it all tastes as good as it looks. Somewhere in between French and Italian, you need to be open to trying unfamiliar ingredients, but you'll definitely be rewarded. Do expect charming service but don't assume the prices are cheap just because you're dining out in bohemian Belleville.
(*1 rue d'Eupatoria, 20ème; +33 9 53 56 24 14; dilia.fr; Tues-Sat for lunch & dinner*)

Parisian Playhouses

Derrière is an unusual restaurant set up like a bohemian Parisian apartment. Guests can dine, drink and flirt in various bedrooms, around a ping-pong table, or in a smoking room through an antique armoire trapdoor.
(*69 rue des Gravilliers, 3ème; +33 1 44 61 91 95; derriere-resto.com; open every day*)

Picture the legendary Beverly Hills Hotel made over into a sexy Parisian party pad and you've got the **Hôtel Grand Amour**. Mingle with music industry and fashion types in the courtyard, and after a bistro-style dinner, don't forget to sneak upstairs in the elevator to the guest floors for a peek at the penis-themed carpet in the hallways. A fun place to start (or end) a girls' or guys' night out.
(*18 rue de la Fidélité, 10e; +33 1 4416 03 30 hotelamourparis.fr/grandamour*). One arrondissement over, the fashionable spot's original older sister **Hôtel Amour** has a lush garden well worth a summer lunch reservation.
(*8 rue de Navarin, 9ème; +33 1 48 78 31 80; hotelamourparis.fr*)

Brooklyn in Paris

Korean fried chicken, absinthe bubble tea and old-school hip-hop over the stereo in a sleekly designed hang-out – **Hero** had me at hello and remains one of my favourite guilty pleasures in Paris. (*289 rue St Denis, 2ème; quixotic-projects.com/venue/hero*). It's one of four spots in the city opened by the same restaurateur group, Quixotic Projects, which always manages to instantly attract the cool kids with quirky Parisian twists on world cuisine, amazing cocktails and out-of-the-box design concepts. Take **Candeleria**, the city's best taco joint, where after dark, through an unmarked door at the back of the room, you can enter a secret world of cocktails laced with chilli and '50s and '60s rock 'n' roll.
(*52 rue de Saintonge, 3ème; quixotic-projects.com/venue/candelaria*).

Or if you're feeling nostalgic for the seaside, around the corner **Le Mary Celeste** and its oyster-shack inspired bar is the perfect fix for 'summer in the city' vibes, with healthy, refreshing tapas plates and natural wines.
(*1 rue Commines, 3ème; +33 9 80 72 98 83; open every day for dinner until 2am*)

Nightcall

Rounding up the Troops

Getting your crew together for drinks and agreeing on the place can often feel a little like herding cats. If you suggest a location on the banks of the Seine, with unobstructed views of the Île Saint-Louis and prices to suit everyone's budget, you might have better luck. **Les Nautes** is housed inside an old customs house near the historic point where Napoleon is said to have first landed in Paris. Take the steps down to the river, where you'll find a large terrace and string lights at the water's edge. When the weather is good and the drinks are flowing, it's the perfect recipe for a good night out. When the weather turns, there's still a sizeable inside bar area where the DJ keeps going until 2am. You can also book the whole thing for private parties.
(*1 Quai des Célestins, 4ème; +33 1 42 74 59 53; Thurs-Sat, 2pm-2am, closes at 7pm Sunday; lesnautes-paris.com*)

Bringing back the house band, **Le Fou** is inspired by early twentieth-century nightlife; sophisticated and civilised on the surface with a place to let loose hiding underground. The ground floor is a masterpiece of 1920s interior design, hosted by hard-working barmen in vintage clinical jackets serving classic cocktails from an art deco bar. Downstairs is the devilish den where the house band, Les Fous Furieux, plays gypsy jazz until 2am.
(*37 bis, rue du Sentier, 2ème; +33 1 40 26 14 94*)

Somewhere between a biker shed and a pirate ship, **Medusa** is a refreshing alternative to pretentious 'mixologist' cocktail bars without slacking on the design and ambience. The staff are laid-back and friendly, and the drinks are good because they're simple. You can even order beer in a can, which is rare in Paris. I'd almost call it a guys' hang-out if those candlelit tables weren't so damn romantic.
(*48 rue Basfroi, 11ème; +33 6 06 98 35 45; open every day, 6pm-2am*)

Decorated like a 1960s Parisian mod's apartment, the lobby of **Le Pigalle**, a party hotel for the hip, has a buzzing restaurant that gets taken over by effortlessly stylish locals after dark. With a DJ and a red velvet pole-dancing lounge, it's the perfect introduction to the cool kids of South Pigalle.
(*9 rue Frochot, 9ème; +33 1 48 78 37 14; open until 2am*)

A drink at **Gravity Bar** is worth the trip; sit at the massive dramatic steel bar and watch it transform into a stage for some very entertaining craft cocktail-making. The kitchen also turns out delicious sharing plates, like salmon bonbons with maple syrup or fried sea snails with aioli.
(*44 rue des Vinaigriers, 10ème; +33 6 98 54 92 49; open Tues-Sat, 7pm-2am*)

Le Pigalle

Round Two (...Three and Four)

Let loose at a rustic Mexican disco frequented by an eclectic crowd of hip Parisians reliving their summers in Tulum. At **La Mano**, the mezcal is flowing and the dance floor is heaving by midnight, as the DJ flip-flops between hip-hop and samba. Book a ceviche dinner before the party really gets going to avoid queues or guest-list woes.
(*10 rue Papillon, 9ème; +33 9 67 50 50 37; Tues-Sat, 8pm-5am*)

Lulu White transports you to a tiny New Orleans speakeasy with passionate bartenders, dark mood lighting and intimate booths tucked away for cosy conversations over an American blues soundtrack. Arrive early or very late to grab a seat in the booths (*12 rue Frochot, 9ème; luluwhite.bar; open every night except Sunday until 4am*). If you need some air after Lulu's absinthe-inspired drinks menu, head down the block to the terrace of **Le Dépanneur lounge** to catch your breath under the string lights (*27 rue Pierre Fontaine, 9ème; ledepanneurpigalle.com; open until 2am*). Soldiering on, across the buzzing *place* (but not for those in search of a quiet glass of wine), is **Le Mansart**, the messy but merry neighbourhood dive bar favoured by Parisian night owls waiting for the trendy midnight clubs of Pigalle to open their doors, most of which are conveniently located within a few minutes' walk. Don't be surprised if you end up heading to the nightclub across the street with some new friends you met while elbowing each other at the bar.
(*1 rue Mansart, 9ème; +33 1 56 92 05 99; open every day until 2am*)

That nightclub across the street is **Le Carmen**. Set in a sumptuous mansion that was once the home of classical composer Georges Bizet and later a high-end brothel, it's a bit like walking into a lavish nineteenth-century courtesan's ball, but with hip-hop and electro music. Dress the part to avoid hassle from the bouncers and arrive early enough to claim your spot in the human-sized birdcage – the best seat in the house.
(*34 rue Duperré, 9ème; le-carmen.fr; open Tues-Sat until 6am; check the Facebook page for DJ sets, live and private events*)

Across town is **Les Bains**, the revived 'Studio 54 of Paris', and the only nightclub in the city with a swimming pool. Before it became an icon of Parisian nightlife, it was Marcel Proust's favourite bath house. In the 1970s, when David Bowie and Mick Jagger were regulars, it was a cultural institution fuelled by sex, drugs, disco and midnight swimming. After years of abandonment, it's back on top as one of the most rock-star nightlife venues in the city (complete with a boutique hotel upstairs). Book dinner in the restaurant and you won't have to worry about the door.
(*7 rue du Bourg l'Abbé, 3ème; +33 1 42 77 07 07, lesBains-Paris.com*)

You can dress much more casually at the **Café de la Presse**, which injects some culture into clubbing with live concerts, international music nights, album release parties, cinema screenings and art exhibitions. Check the Facebook page to see the party programme.
(*36 boulevard de la Bastille, 12ème; facebook.com/cafedelapresseparis; open every day, on weekends until 5am*)

Secret Discos

For the more adventurous party crowd, **La Java** is a nightclub nearing a century old, hidden inside an art deco arcade in a less glitzy part of town. This underground dancehall is where Edith Piaf and Django Reinhardt played some of their first gigs in the 1920s. At that time, the melting pot of different cultures arriving in Paris had given birth to an urban accordion-based style of music called *bal musette*, and with it came a new fast waltz dance they called *la java*. Fast forward to present-day Paris, this now uber-kitsch nightclub hasn't exactly

La Java

decided what it wants to be as it approaches its hundredth year. Sometimes it's a live tango night that come 1am turns into an electro-swing club until dawn. Other nights it's an all welcome LGBT dress-up club. Expect the unexpected and prepare for a very atypical evening, which is exactly why the curious, slightly bored, gilded Parisian *jeunesse* are passing through its doors once again.
(*105 rue du Faubourg du Temple, 10ème; La-Java.fr; see the website or Facebook page for programme and opening hours*)

Your first time at **L'Orphée** is a bit like tagging along to a party where you haven't met the host. Get your fix of R&B and hip-hop at this speakeasy nightclub/apartment by finding the unmarked entrance at 7 *rue Pierre Fontaine* and entering the first apartment door on the left. Weeknights at L'Orphée are preferable to the weekends, and just like any house party, arrive fashionably late in the night.
(*7 rue Pierre Fontaine, 9ème; +33 1 42 80 24 38; Tues-Sat, 8pm-2am*)

Hiding away in a cobblestone backstreet of the 3rd arrondissement, an old-fashioned tango dancehall still teaches couple's classes from 6pm but turns into one of the coolest LGBT hotspots in Paris from 10.30pm onwards. If kitsch decor, an international fashion crowd and dancing your butt off to Rihanna all night sounds like your scene, **Tango (La Boîte à Frissons)** should be right up your alley.
(*13 rue au Maire, 3ème; boite-a-frissons.fr; open Fri & Sun until 5am, Sun until 11pm*)

The Parisian House Party

There's just something so much more memorable about losing your balance and spilling your red wine in a Haussmanian walk-up cluttered with antiques and bric-a-brac from the flea markets. When I first moved to Paris, I quickly found out that the real nightlife was not just in the bars or in the clubs but in the Parisian apartments. At first I wasn't sure how I was going to get invited to one, but sure enough, if we break away from that whole 'single foreigners alone together' thing, meeting just one local can gain us access into Parisian apartments for an entire season...

The Dos and Don'ts

- **Do** bring your own bottle of wine. Natural wines are most appreciated, but if you're stuck, something around €8 with a nice-looking label from the Monoprix supermarket is always perfectly acceptable. Remember to remove the price tag.

- **Don't** bring an entourage, not even a small one. Check with the host if you can bring a plus-one.

- **Do** try to speak French at first, no matter how rusty you are, just to let people know you're making an effort. They'll find it charming and let you finish your sentence in English anyway.

- **Don't** shake hands with guests or try to hug people.

- **Do** remember to dab a good perfume or cologne under your ears. When you're introduced to fellow party guests who initiate *la bise* (French cheek kissing), make the kisses quick but gentle and most importantly dry; one on each cheek.

- **Don't** interrupt the evening's ambience by trying to do *la bise* with everyone in a room full of people you don't know. Be selective with your kisses; it's actually very Parisian.

- **Do** compliment the host on a nice piece of vintage furniture. Chances are it's a flea market find of which they're very proud.

- **Don't** wear stiletto heels that will scuff the wood parquet and be cause for neighbour noise complaints (the greatest hazard for throwing parties in Paris).

- **Do** make an effort to look like you haven't made an effort. This also happens to be the secret to Parisian style.

06

I Know This Great Little Place...

Hi Nessy,

A few weeks ago I took the leap and moved to Paris. I'm still settling in, finding my own rhythm in a new neighbourhood, figuring out which boulangerie is going to be my regular, which café serves the best coffee – just the basics for now. I thought I'd have a little more time, but my oldest friend has just booked a trip to come and check in on me. I'm panicking because I had this idea that by the time I'd start receiving visitors, I'd already be savvy enough to lead them around like a local to hidden gems and know all the stories behind them. So I was wondering if I might be able to borrow a few of your secret spots? In a nutshell, I need a crash course in looking like a local and I thought you'd be the best person to ask.

In gratitude,
Lindsay
(also hoping to call myself a Parisian someday soon)

Parisians like to lay claim to their favourite hidden spots – the ones that they 'unexpectedly stumbled across one day'. We like to feel as if we've discovered a forgotten corner of the capital. It's all part of being a Parisian. If you stay long enough, you'll no doubt end up with your own list of urban secrets. But what sets you apart from those just passing through is creating great memories wherever you plant your little flag. So who better than your oldest friend to create those first memories with and help you transition through the 'I just moved to Paris' phase? To point you in the right direction with the limited time you have together, I'm going to pass on some of my own secret addresses where I've spent some of my most memorable moments in this city so far. They should have you feeling like locals together in no time.

French Village Life

Country Bumpkin Lane

Just off the main shopping street of a residential neighbourhood in the 14th arrondissement, tucked away ever so sneakily you could almost miss it, is *rue des Thermopyles*, a heavenly Parisian countryside hideaway. Vines curl around peeling pastel window shutters and arches of thick green foliage wildly frame the cobblestone path as if they were portals to a remote French village. Follow the *rue des Thermopyles* to the end and you'll come across a local garden for picnics on the *pelouse* or a first date on the benches. On the other side is la **Cité Bauer**, where neighbours sit and chat on their doorsteps, exchanging gardening tips. The prize for the most unusual façade most certainly goes to No. 19 Cité Bauer, for its impressive sculpted heart-shaped door. The words '*Isten Hozott*' are inscribed into the ironwork inside the heart, which means 'welcome' in Hungarian. The house was in fact built in 1959 by a Hungarian artist, Alexandre Mezei. If you have some extra time on your hands, take a five-minute detour to **Villa d'Alesia** nearby, where you'll find another charming street dotted with a beautiful line-up of art deco façades, mostly ateliers, one of which belonged to Henri Matisse.

(*Start your stroll at rue des Thermophyles, 14ème*)

Rue des Thermophyles,
Country Bumpkin Lane

The Other Montmartre

For an undiscovered tourist-free alternative to Montmartre (the cupcake hilltop village of Paris), escape to a different corner of the city in the 20th arrondissement with just as much charm and just as many steps. In an undisturbed corner of the French capital known officially and affectionately, as **La Campagne à Paris** (the countryside in Paris), think of it as a smaller, secret Montmartre. Built on a hill between 1907 and 1926, the roads that wind up to the top are connected by picturesque staircases that shortcut past enviable backyards. Every house is different and residents put their all into their patios, decorating them with garden gnomes and miniature windmills. There's even a local grocery store just like Amélie's, on *rue du Capitaine Ferber*, and old-fashioned storefronts with gorgeous typography. As for a preferred scenic route? I don't have one. Dive down every staircase, poke your head round every gate and get absolutely positively lost on this leafy little hill.
(*Use rue Irénée Blanc as a starting point, 20ème*)

While you're in the area, stop for lunch in a nearby twelfth-century village of the 20th arrondissement at **Café Lumière**.
(*15 rue Saint-Blaise, 20ème; +33 9 5058 76 86; open every day, 10.30am-midnight*)

Brocante by Day and Bistro by Night

Eva Pritsky couldn't really decide whether it wanted to sell antiques or entertain guests, so this tiny fairy-lit hodgepodge of psychedelic chic does both. You'll sit and drink and be merry on the eclectic furniture of the brocante, catch an impromptu live guitar set – maybe even make an offer on that kitschy 1950s love seat you've been perched on all night. Mix with the locals and regulars, artists and antique dealers in this warm and nostalgic brocante moonlighting as a café. (*5, rue d'Eupatoria, 20ème; +33 1 44 62 20 69; Tues-Sat, 5pm-2am; check the Facebook page for events: facebook.com/Eva.Pritsky*)

Secret Sunday Brunching in Saint-Germain

Looking like the perfect tea salon on a village road, **L'Heure Gourmande** has the most underrated Sunday tables waiting in a hidden cobblestone passage. Try the Provençale quiches served with generous well-dressed salads, and if you have room, order the outstanding chocolate tart for dessert. The pace is slow, the kitchen is small and the ingredients are so fresh you'll wonder if they don't have their own garden patch nearby.
(*22 Passage Dauphine, 6ème; +33 1 46 34 00 40; open every day, 12pm-7pm*)

Parisian Cottages

Experience what life would be like living in a village of Parisian cottages and lose yourself in the little-known neighbourhood of **Quartier Mouzaïa**, a labyrinth of leafy alleys built on an old gypsum quarry. Beneath your feet is a maze of

Left: L'Heure Gourmande
Overleaf: Cité Florale

excavated galleries, making it unlikely that larger modern buildings could ever be built on this land. Imagine how precious this haven of nineteenth-century cottages will be in a hundred years. (*Find my favourite cottages: Villla des Lilas, Villa Loraine at the end of rue de l'Egalité, on the left and Villa de Bellevue. Oh, and don't miss the ones on rue de la liberté, 19ème*)

A Little-Known Paris Vineyard

The quiet hilltop village of **Butte Bergeyre** is accessible by three staircases or a single winding road. Once you reach the very top of the stairs at 100 metres altitude, a very special view of Montmartre in the distance awaits, with a halo of sunlight perfectly centred over the *Sacré-Cœur* if you catch a good sunset. You'll be so taken with the view that, like me, it might take you several minutes to realise that there's a vineyard right under your nose. Located just minutes from the gates of the well-known *Parc des Buttes Chaumont*, most Parisians I've asked aren't even aware of its existence. It belongs to the city of Paris and produces around 130 half-litre bottles a year, which is not very much, so it doesn't go on sale, but a few in-the-know Parisians are lucky enough to sample the rosé at the *Fête des Jardins* (pg. 82), an annual open celebration day for public and not-so-public gardens. To the left of your view over the vines, you'll find the shared neighbourhood vegetable garden, where they grow tomatoes in all shapes, sizes and colours. On Wednesday and Sunday afternoons you can walk right in and make yourself at home, even have a picnic if you like. There's an olive tree and a row of beehives in the back, and some great little hiding places. Once covered in seventeenth-century windmills, the Butte Bergeyre was briefly the site of a family amusement park in the early 1900s and hosted the principal stadium for the Olympic Games in 1924, before making way for a residential neighbourhood inaugurated by Josephine Baker in 1927.

(*Hilltop staircase access at 21 rue Manin or via rue Michel Tagrine; vineyard viewpoint and veggie garden at the angle of rue Georges Lardennois and rue Remy de Gourmont*)

City of Flowers

The 13th arrondissement in the east of Paris might just be the most overlooked arrondissement of them all. It's filled with treasures like the **Butte-aux-Cailles** – a French countryside town within the city – endless art deco architecture, some wonderful street art and Paris's quietest micro-village, the **Cité Florale**. As you wander through its tranquil cobblestone streets, with botanical names like *rue des Iris* or *rue des Orchidées*, you'll almost want to speak in a whisper.
(*rue des Iris, 13ème*)

South of France in the Marais

Take a time out from city life and wander into the ***Place du Marché Sainte Catherine***, a piece of Provence where you most need it, hidden in the heart of

the Marais. It used to be a medieval market square, now it's a cheerful hideout resembling a village piazza surrounded by café terraces. Any of the benches are good for a coffee break to watch the world go by.
(*Access via rue Caron, 4ème*)

The Locals' Terrace of Montmartre

Perched at the top of a picturesque staircase, away from the tourists, the café terrace of **L'Eté en Pente Douce** is a rare slice of authentic Montmartre worth seeking out in the maze of streets winding up the hill.
(*8 rue Paul Albert, 18ème; +33 1 42 64 02 67; open every day from midday to midnight*)

Eat like a Local

In Paris, everyone has their own 'QG', short for *quartier general*; it literally means 'headquarters', but we're really just talking about a restaurant, bar or café where we like to hang out a lot – where we probably know the owner's name and what to order without looking at the menu. So you can say, *C'est mon QG* (pronounced 'quoo-jeh'), in much the same way as you talk about your 'local' spot.

The Last of the Trucker Bars

They don't accept credit cards here, but it's more fun to watch them ring up that old antique cash register anyway. **Chez Léon** is one of the city's last two '*routiers*' – what the French call a truckers' bar – a traditional bistro where off-duty truck drivers used to go for a comforting home-cooked meal in the city, drink with colleagues and share tales of their travels. This one has been around since 1910, and it shows. Formica tables, chequered tablecloths, kitschy crockery, roadside memorabilia on the walls; the place is a time machine to French working-class dining establishments of the past. It's been owned by the same adorable family since 1960, serving up their homemade shepherd's pie, pot au feu, roast beef, apple herring and other warming classics that are all washed down perfectly with a carafe of the house red.

You won't find many truckers here these days, however. They stopped coming after the closure of Les Halles, the legendary food market that was once the beating heart of Paris. The city's tolerance had run out for the daily parade of giant lorries passing through the centre of town. Today, young professionals and long-time residents of the *quartier* claim this old truckers' bistro as their Q.G.. It doesn't get more local, heart-warming and French than Chez Léon.
(*5 rue de l'Isly, 8ème; Mon-Sat for lunch & dinner; no reservations*)

Mom and Pop Run the Kitchen

Au Coin de Malte is an honest French neighbourhood bistro with real food,

real people, and real good prices. A great mood-booster, this place has so much heart, and on Fridays they always have a live band.
(*1 rue de Malte, 11ème; +33 1 43 55 19 52; open Mon- Fri for dinner*)

Wine and Dine in a Hidden Passage

I dream about the garlicky razor clams in breadcrumbs served at **Coinstot Vino**, a humble *cave à manger* that set up shop inside the time-travelling maze of the *Passage des Panoramas*. An evening of natural wine discovery awaits you under the glass roof of the Belle Époque arcade, where you can feast *en terrasse* with the merry crowd of local winos until the passage reluctantly closes its gates after midnight. Just make sure you don't get locked inside – although wouldn't that be an evening to remember!
(*26bis Passage des Panoramas, 2ème; +33 1 44 82 08 54; Mon-Sat for lunch & dinner*)

Armenian Soul Food at a Secret Restaurant

La Maison De La Culture Arménienne is the sort of place that you only hear about via word of mouth. I heard about it from a guy in a bar one night and went in search of his vague promise of a 'secret Armenian gem' near the métro Cadet the next day. There is absolutely zero indication of a restaurant behind the street entrance at 17 *rue Bleue*, just a door with a keypad. Don't panic, there's no code; just push the button at the bottom, wait for the door to click, and let yourself in. Head to the back of the courtyard, past the bamboos, veer left, and look for the Armenian and French flags swaying together above the doorway marked Maison de la Culture Arménienne. You've found it.

Follow the comforting smell of simmering onions and spices up to the first floor, where you'll find the warmest welcome in Paris. You've never met Tchinar, but she'll greet you as if you were part of her own family stopping in for a home-cooked meal. Tchinar is *la patronne* and she runs this place while her husband mans the kitchen. Just like at home, there's no menu, but your newly adopted Mama Armenia will suggest the dishes of the day, which always include their special recipe for juicy meat dumplings, an ancient comfort food, that was carried across Central Asia along the Silk Road by nomadic horsemen as early as the thirteen century. Order both variations of the house dumplings and another traditional plate such as stuffed aubergine or smoked spicy chicken.

Humbly decorated with trinkets alluding to their Armenian roots, this restaurant will tug at your heartstrings. The rustic but noble canteen feels lost in time and place. We could be dining circa 1980 in a Soviet country, which indeed Armenia was until the early '90s. The food is made with love and pride, for the modest sum of €8-€10 per person.
(*17 rue Bleue, 9ème; +33 1 48 24 63 89; Mon-Sat for lunch, 12pm-3pm, dinner, 7pm-11pm*)

Left: Au Coin de Malte

Below: Homemade dumplings in a secret restaurant, Maison de la culture Arménienne

Get Your French Soul Food on

I like to sit at the bar of **Le Chat Ivre** and watch the wine being swirled and the cheese being sliced. Run by a father and son team, this is a vibrant, locally loved spot in the backstreets of Bastille, with comforting French tapas plates at good

prices, beautiful wine and family-style service. It's also one of the few places in Paris I'll order *l'Os à Moelle* (bone marrow), generously sprinkled with garlic breadcrumbs and living up to its reputation as a French delicacy.
(*22 rue des Taillandiers, 11ème; +33 1 43 55 77 08; open every evening until midnight*)

Lunch on the Métro

Metropolitain is a small restaurant with a small menu and small wine list – but what a grand experience. Decorated like an old métro platform with a charming garden out back, the prices are as friendly as the staff but the food wouldn't be out of place in a Michelin star chef's kitchen.
(*8 rue de Jouy, 4ème; +33 9 81 20 37 38; open Mon-Sat*)

The House on the Corner

Le Temps de Cerises is one of the last little houses of bygone Paris still standing in the heart of the city, and thanks to its unchanging eighteenth-century mosaic façade, the traditional French bistro earned itself the title of a historical monument. Inside, we could be stepping back in time fifty years, when the same photographs hung on the wall and the same old clock chimed on the hour, as if any of the regulars were ever in a rush to leave this timeless place. You'll find the menu very friendly, even for the fussiest eaters.
(*31 rue de la Cerisaie, 4ème; +33 1 42 72 08 63*)

Right: Au Petit Fer à Cheval
Page 133: Les Grands Serres

The Tiny Horseshoe Bar

Cute as a button and about as small as a button, stop into **Au Petit Fer à Cheval** after a busy day shopping in Le Marais. The decor hasn't changed at this century-old Parisian brasserie, with its unique horseshoe shaped bar. Locals know there's a hidden dining room at the back, perfect for a quiet bistro lunch away from the crowds. If you go for dinner, while you're waiting for a table pop into the wine bar inside the bookshop across the street (pg. 35) and browse the shelves over a glass of vino.

(*30 rue Vieille du Temple, 4ème; +33 1 42 72 47 47; open every day, 9am-2am*)

Best Boeuf Bourguignon in Town

To get a taste of the classic old-world Parisian bistro without the cheesy tourist atmosphere and snooty service, try **Chez Paul**. Order adventurously; you won't regret it, and the waitress is happy to explain every last ingredient. Authentic, romantic and unpretentious, don't worry about reserving – you can usually find a table for two on the terrace before 8pm.

(*13 rue de Charonne, 11ème; chezpaul.com; open every day, 12pm-12.30am*)

Secret Spaghetti

It looks like an ordinary Italian deli selling panini sandwiches on a bustling market street in Saint-Germain, but it's hiding a secret. In a shadowy corner at the back of this family owned shop, indicated only by a blackboard next to the cash register, disappear past the displays of Italian produce and climb the old spiral staircase to find **L'Etage**, a lovely little restaurant with the ambience of a cosy apartment. Jazz music plays softly in the background and the menu is written entirely in Italian (which the rather handsome waiters kindly translate and poetically explain to you, item by item). All the ingredients are sourced from Italy and the recipes come straight from the family's grandmother.

(*First floor above La Bottega Pastavino, 18 rue de Buci, 6ème; +33 1 44 07 09 56; open Mon-Sat for lunch & dinner*)

A Sixteenth-Century Apéro

At the foot of one of the most beautiful, almost-medieval buildings in Paris, book a table *en terrasse* at **Les Fines Gueules** for an evening of Parisian people-watching while enjoying the freshest charcuterie, their legendary tuna tartare and superb cheese. Let them recommend you something from their organic wine list; the folks couldn't be friendlier and might even let you tour of their incredible underground *cave à vins* after dinner if you ask. Open until midnight, you can also just swing by the bar for a quick wine tasting and nibbles.

(*43 rue Croix des Petits Champs, 1er, +33 1 42 61 35 41; lesfinesgueules.fr, open every day for lunch from 12pm & dinner from 7pm*)

The Jungles of Paris

Tomb Raider's Day off

If Indiana Jones ever wound up in Paris waiting for his next adventure, I'd expect you could find him at **Les Grands Serres**, gazing out from his cave over the tropical jungle next to the Seine. For four hundred years, these Parisian greenhouses have been part of the *Jardin des Plantes*, an unparalleled scientific institution in eighteenth-century Europe. Wander through the series of four giant greenhouses, including a unique art deco one, and discover the different landscapes and temperatures, from the mangrove swamps to the cactus forest, with a rainforest in between. An ideal place for tomb raiders to unwind on their day off in the city.

(Allée Becquerel, Jardin des Plantes, 5ème; +33 1 40 79 56 01; entry €6; open every day 10am-6pm, closed Tues. Don't miss the cabinet of curiosities next door, pg. 74)

My Secret Champs-Élysées Garden

Duck and dive through the army of shoppers on the Champs-Élysées and accelerate past the chaotic roundabout, turning right onto *avenue Franklin Roosevelt*. After 200 metres, as you approach the river, with the Eiffel Tower poking its head out over the trees, spot the marble sculpture nestled in the bushes on your left, which looks as if it might be hiding a lost world behind it. This means you've found **Jardin de la Nouvelle France**, formerly known as the Garden of the Swiss Valley. Just a few steps further along, camouflaged in the greenery, you'll find a little gate. Head down the higgledy-piggledy steps and through the arch to find something pretty close to paradise. Suddenly, the noise of bustling Paris and the screeching traffic are silenced and replaced with the sound of softly trickling water. You're cocooned by evergreens, bamboo, lilacs, maples and ivy. There are water lilies, a century-old weeping beech tree and wild flowers that smell like buttermilk. Monet should have painted this place. The pond is home to an otter who surfaces occasionally and to carp that glide in slow motion through the water. It's amazing how many people walk past that little green gate, totally unaware of the urban treasure that lies behind it. Our little secret.

(Corner of avenue Franklin Roosevelt and Cours de la Reine, 8ème; always open)

Sunday Bird Bazaar

From Monday to Saturday, one of Paris's last flower markets can be found on the same island as Notre Dame Cathedral, but on Sundays, the birds arrive at the **Marché aux Fleurs et Oiseaux**. I don't know how this place still exists, but you'll find exotic parrots, cheerful canaries and beautiful birdcages to take them home in. If a live bird is not on your shopping list, they do have an abundance of baby cactus variations for decorating the windowsill.

(Find it on Sundays where Place Louis Lépine meets Quai de la Corse, 4ème)

Under the Banana Tree

Of all my discoveries while attempting to get some exercise, **Le Jardin des Soupirs** is a personal favourite, found while running out of breath down a picturesque pedestrian passage in the 20th arrondissement. It's nothing short of an urban paradise, and it is maintained by local residents. Picture a winding path through vegetable patches, water running under a little bridge, and tables and chairs for picnics next to the banana tree.

(*18 Passage des Soupirs; Sat, 11am-1pm, Sunday, 4pm-8pm*)

Paris's Park in the Sky

If you were under the impression that New York's much-adored High Line was a unique feature to the Big Apple, take one of the staircases up to an old railway bridge in the 12th arrondissement, and you'll find the original High Line, **La Promenade Plantée**. Built sixteen years before the New York promenade, Paris's own railway park actually served as the model and inspiration for its American counterpart. The elevated pathway stretches for almost 5 kilometres across the 12th arrondissement, following the route of the retired *ligne de Vincennes* railway track from Bastille to the *boulevard Périphérique* beltway that borders the city. Ten metres above ground with the treetops, you'll have eye-level views through the windows of some of Paris's most beautiful apartments.

(*Access via staircases starting from the corner of rue de Lyon & ave Daumesnil, 12ème*)

Secret Paris Enclaves

The Hidden Antiques Village of the Marais

A rickety old chair on a backstreet between the Marais and the Seine marks a hidden entrance to **Village Saint-Paul**, where a small community of antique dealers hold court in their own mini citadel of treasure. Weekend brocante sales reminiscent of summers in Provence are frequent, and you can score anything from medieval trinkets to 1970s retro barware.

(*3 rue Charlemagne, 4ème; check the calendar for special brocante market days on levillagesaintpaul.com/calendrier*)

Hunt for a Rose Garden

It took me several years of Sunday strolls in the Marais to discover **Le Square Saint-Gilles Grand Veneur – Pauline-Roland** (long-winded, I know) hidden at the end of a series of residential courtyards within courtyards in a maze of backstreets. In the right season, roses climb the trellises overlooked by a beautiful *hôtel particulier*. The roses are a dedication to Pauline Roland, a writer for one of the Paris's first feminist newspapers.

(*Hint: find the rue du Grand Veneur, 3ème*)

A Private View of the Eiffel Tower

The Eiffel Tower and I like playing peekaboo with each other. I find unexpected views of her all across the city. Find one of my secret vistas of the iron lady in a hidden art nouveau enclave called **Square Rapp**.

(*Off avenue Rapp, 7ème*)

A Beautiful Dump

I found this hidden Paris enclave by accident while driving around on my Mobylette, utterly lost in the one-way system of the 9th arrondissement. I think I literally had sparkles in my eyes when I drove inside. In the 1970s, **Cité de Trévise** was used as a public dumping ground by local inhabitants, filled with car bonnets and broken household appliances. One day, a man who lived nearby decided to clean it up all on his own. Touched by what he had done, the locals stopped leaving their rubbish in the square and several years later a group of gardeners spruced up the park that surrounds the regal fountain to this day.

(*Find the Cité de Trévise in the 9ème arrondissement hidden behind rue Richer*)

A Theatrical Hiding Place

Well hidden, minutes from the Opéra Garnier in the busiest area of Paris, the **Édouard VII Square** should be as bustling as a Roman piazza, attracting tourists to marvel at its elegant architecture, but you can have this majestic urban hideaway to yourself. Turn off the bustling *boulevard Capucines* at No. 18

and follow the pedestrian road to discover what looks like the inside of an amphitheatre with a Haussmanian twist. Centre stage is the statue of the English monarch King Edward VII, a favourite guest amongst fashionable Parisian society during the Belle Époque. He loved French fashion and can take credit for the creation of the three-piece suit, which he had tailored in Paris at his request. A great patron of the arts, he also spent a lot of time at the theatre, notably pursuing the beautiful French actress Sarah Bernhardt backstage. After the King's death, the city of Paris built this sequestered enclave in his honour and made it home to the **Théâtre Edouard VII**, one of the capital's most romantic venues to catch a show. This theatre even has English subtitles that get projected above the stage, thanks to **Theatre in Paris** (*theatreinparis.com*), a cultural start-up that's opening the doors of French theatre to anglophones.

On your way out of the square, don't miss a second enclave through the arches behind the rear of Edward's statue, where you'll find the perfume atelier of Fragonard.
(*Édouard VII Square, 9ème*)

Above: Édouard VII Square
Right: Square Rapp

Page 137
Left: Design & Nature
Right: Newspaper Kiosk

135

Small Shops & Time-Travelling Retail Therapy

Curiosity Cabinets

I'm not entirely convinced that when the clock strikes midnight, the creatures in the window of **Design & Nature** don't come alive. Behind the stunning *Place des Victoires*, this taxidermy shop will stop you in your tracks. They also specialise in rare skeletons and mythological Minotaur-esque taxidermy.

(*4 rue d'Aboukir, 2ème; designetnature.fr; Mon-Fri, 10am-7pm, Sat, 11am-7pm*)

If the art of stuffed beasts is your bag, don't miss the church of Paris taxidermy, **Deyrolles**, a legendary curiosity cabinet since 1831 and a favourite Parisian hang-out of indie film director Wes Anderson.

(*46 rue du Bac, 7ème; deyrolle.com; Mon-Sat, 10am-7pm, closes for lunch on Mondays*)

Very close by, on *rue Jacob*, is **Librairie Alain Brieux**, a lesser-known but equally rewarding cabinet of curiosities specialising in medical and rare anatomy ephemera, historical scientific instruments and antique botanical prints.

(*48 rue Jacob, 6ème; alainbrieux.com; Mon-Fri, 10am-6.30pm, Sat, 2pm-6.30pm, daily lunchtime closing between 1pm-2pm*)

For more morbid anatomy, don't miss the incredible room full of skeletons in the old palaeontology building (*Galeries d'Anatomie comparée et de Paléontologie*) at the **Natural History Museum** (pg. 74).

Finally, let's see if you don't find a forgotten object from your childhood at the **Tombée du Camion** (literally meaning 'fallen off the truck'). This hoarder's boutique is filled with an abundance of unusual and strange bits and bobs, from toy doll parts to vintage café ashtrays.

(*17 rue Joseph de Maistre, 18ème; tombeesducamion.com; open every day, 1pm-8pm*)

Aladdin's Caves

Founded in 1818 and now one of the oldest shops in the city, **A l'Oriental** is a Parisian treasure chest of antique smoking pipes. Nestled amongst the boutiques of Palais Royale, it could easily moonlight as a tiny museum dedicated to the gentleman's essential accessory of yesteryear.

(*19/21 Galerie de Chartres, Palais-Royal, 1er; aloriental.canalblog.com; Mon-Fri, 9am-6pm, closes at lunchtime*)

In the heart of the 11th arrondissement, the Oberkampf district has its own mini Paris flea market; a petite shopping village of mid-century design, decorative arts and vintage lighting waiting behind the weathered façades of the neighbourhood's old ateliers. **Belle Lurette** is a favourite with prop-hunters and a perfect opportunity to combine shopping and lazy-day strolls.

(*5 rue du Marché Popincourt, 11ème; bellelurette.eu; Tues-Sun, 12pm-7pm on weekdays & from 2pm on weekends*)

On the sidewalk of *boulevard Saint-Michel*, you'll find an old Parisian newspaper kiosk turned **Vintage Camera Shop**. The shopkeeper of this tiny makeshift boutique is there most days of the week and has a truly stunning collection of antique photography equipment, most of it still in perfect working condition. (*Newspaper Kiosk at 25 boulevard Saint-Michel, 6ème*)

Incredible beaded furniture, charming tableware, colourful wax prints, unique Malian jewellery, nostalgic matchboxes; **Boutique Csao** is a vibrant little bazaar of African crafts. Since the '90s, this store has celebrated the work of Senegalese and West African artisans, sourcing some seriously charming household decor while exercising fair trade and encouraging sustainable development back home. (*9 rue Elzévir, 3ème; csao.fr; Tues-Sat, 11am-7pm, opens at 2pm on Sun & Mon*)

Digging through archives in the **Marché Dauphine** is addictive. You can lose hours here flicking through 1950s pocket guides, vintage luggage labels and even 1930s pornography that's rather difficult to ignore. I do most of my rummaging upstairs on the first floor, specifically the stands between No. 211 and 218. (*134 rue des Rosiers, 93400 Marché aux Puces de Saint-Ouen; Métro: Porte de Clignancourt; marche-dauphine.com; open Fri mornings, and Sat-Mon, 9.30am-6pm*)

While you're at the Paris flea market, make sure not to miss the *Marché Vernaison* and *Marché Paul Bert* (pg. 49).*

Window shopping on your way up to Montmartre just isn't complete without checking in on the very photogenic **L'Objet qui Parle** – as the name suggests, its curious objects really do speak to you.
(*86 rue des Martyrs, 18ème; +33 6 09 67 05 30; Mon-Sat, 1pm-7.30pm*)

*Also see La Galcante on pg. 71.

Get Out of Town

Escape from Paris? Yes, sometimes even the truest Parisphile needs a break from the romance of this limestone jungle in exchange for some country air...

From Paris to Provence

Picture a quaint French village you can reach in time for lunch, where you can have a table for two in a sun-drenched garden with hens crowing next door. Too much to ask? Not in **Barbizon**, nestled at the edge of the picturesque Fontainebleau Forest, less than an hour's drive from Paris. It's the kind of village you might see in a Renoir painting – in fact, this village practically gave birth to French Impressionist art. Both Claude Monet and Pierre-Auguste Renoir came here in the 1800s as young Parisian art students, lured by the bucolic charms of Barbizon that influenced them to develop their own art movement, which we now call Impressionism. Artistry is still very much alive in this village, peppered with ateliers and galleries tucked away down cobblestone paths.
(*Renting a car recommended. For public transport, take the RER D train which runs every thirty minutes to Melun and then a short taxi ride into Barbizon, 77630*)

If you don't have the means to leave town but still crave that southern French summer feeling, I've got just the fix. At **Le Sud**, your table awaits surrounded by olive trees, Provençale pottery, rattan chairs, rustic plates and the aromas of authentic southern cuisine. Find this unexpected dose of sunshine behind the dull concrete of Le Palais de Congrès concert hall in the 17th arrondissement. It's sort of like dining on the set of a TV show in a Provençale village, except the olive and orange trees are very much real thanks to the natural sunlight coming through the glass roof. The effort they've gone to in recreating Provence right here in Paris will charm you as much as the country-bumpkin specialities on the menu.
(*91 boulevard Gouvion-Saint-Cyr, 17ème; +33 1 45 74 02 77; open every day, 8am-11.30pm*)

Barbizon

A Parisian Wonderland

Paris might already have Euro Disneyland, but I know a little place away from the crowds that's more like the real thing. If Alice had chosen a bright yellow door at the end of the rabbit hole and if the Mad Hatter had in fact been a legendary clown from Soviet Russia (I'll explain in a moment), Lewis Carroll's *Adventures in Wonderland* could have easily taken place at **Le Moulin Jaune**. An hour's drive south-east from the steps of Notre Dame, on the Grand Morin River (*Seine et Marne*), lies a lemon-yellow castle and its enchanting gardens.

This is the French residence of Slava Polunin, 'avant-garde performance artist' and 'the world's supreme clown'. He grew up in Communist Russia, looks a little like Father Christmas, and dreams up ideas for his shows and festivals while lying on an antique bed that floats down the Marne River through his property. The Dali-meets-Disney wonderland consists of: five kaleidoscopic gardens with book trees; flower beds to sleep in; a giant egg house for chickens; a river that flows backwards; a gypsy caravan paradise; a capsized ship café; floating musical moons; horses with pink wings, and a temple brought over from Korea by Buddhist monks. And that's not the whole list. Le Moulin Jaune is an ever-changing playful environment that has to be seen to be believed. (*Open days listed on moulinjaune.com; reservations via Maison du Tourisme du Pays Créçois, +33 1 64 63 70 19, tourisme@payscrecois.net*)

Right: Provins
Opposite: Murs à pêches

Medieval Time-Capsule Town

So you've been to Paris a few times and seen Versailles, done the
Chartres Cathedral and been to Monet's Giverny. **Provins** is a walled
medieval town and a UNESCO World Heritage site that's perfect for a
Sunday escape from the city. You can easily do this trip without a car
by taking one of the suburban RER trains from Gare de l'Est to Provins
(1h25 mins), and then a minibus to the town centre.
(*€18 on the RER or Navigo Pass accepted; schedules on transilien.com*)

The Last Peach Orchards of Paris

Peaches grown right here in Paris? Centuries ago, Paris produced up
to 17 million of the fuzzy fruits a year, and even today, a little-known
community of cultivators is still growing them in the very same
orchards, known as the **Murs à pêches**. These were the original greenhouses.
Built during the seventeenth century, a 600-kilometre maze of walls and
agricultural plots provided a unique and unlikely microclimate for the
fruit, normally suited for cultivation in warmer areas.

The Parisian *pêchers* of Montreuil once supplied peaches for the court
of Versailles and French nobility. Even the Queen of England, the Prince
of Wales and Russian Tsars came to the peach orchards of Montreuil to
taste the unique varieties of Parisian peaches. The industry reached its
peak in the 1870s and as the Industrial Age loomed, the production of
Parisian peaches went into decline. The arrival of cheaper produce on
the market saw the orchards disappear into the urban fabric.

Today, only 17 kilometres of deteriorating walls remain standing
and visible from the original maze that was once the celebrated *Murs
à pêches*. Despite the endless pressure of urbanisation, there are local
associations fighting for the protection and resurrection of this historic
farming culture. Thanks to the restoration efforts so far, the orchards

are an unexpected and beautiful urban anomaly, largely undiscovered by most Parisians. With the Eiffel Tower peering over the walls in the distance, the historical *Murs à pêches* make for a wonderful Sunday discovery. Doors are open to the public every week.

(*The main access points are at the Impasse Gobétue at 23 rue Saint-Just, 93100 Montreuil; open every Sunday afternoon and the Jardin d'École, 4 rue Jardin, open every second Sunday of the month, except in August*)

07

Parents are Coming to Town

Bonjour Nessy,

I was wondering if I could ask for your help. I'm soon to be hitched to my French boyfriend and my parents are coming over to meet him and his family for the first time. They haven't been to Paris since their honeymoon, and this time they're bringing my younger siblings with them. I don't want to put all the planning on my fiancé's shoulders but I could use some expert advice (that's you) to make this trip go as smoothly as possible. I'm in need of a few family bonding activities and kid-friendly restaurants. As a long-time reader of the blog, I know you also fell in with a Parisian and I'm wondering where you had your first 'meet the parents' dinner. If you have any special tips, I promise to make a toast to you at our wedding!

Merci mille fois,
Eva

Hopefully this will be the first of many more visits to Paris for your family, so let's make them feel at home here as much as possible. Rather than treating them like tourists and dragging them around town to all the sights, why not allow your loved ones to picture themselves actually living here, doing the same things Parisian families do? Put yourself in their shoes and cater to their comfort zones while gently introducing them to the things you love most about Paris. As for the kids, well I'm basically still one myself, so I have a few ideas up my sleeve...

For the Jazz-Obsessed Dad

Somewhere to tap his feet

Tucked behind two of Paris's most iconic sidewalk cafés in Saint-Germain, the name says it all: **Chez Papa**. Dad will feel right at home listening to the live jazz in this cosy, candlelit old-school joint. Spread out over two storeys, the grand piano centrepiece of the bar is accompanied by a talented roster of bassists, trumpeters and vocalists. Jazz starts around 9pm. Make an evening of it by reserving a table for dinner or drinks.

(*3 rue Saint-Benoît, 6ème; +33 1 42 86 99 63; open Tues-Sun; check Jazzclubchezpapa. free.fr to see what's on the programme*)

A Speakeasy in the Paris of the East

Picture yourself in Shanghai in the 1930s, a city of sin filled with smoky underground cabarets and intoxicating jazz music ringing out into the night. Three to four nights a week, the underground cabaret of **Le China Club** opens its red doors for a cinematic evening of live music. The programme is eclectic and always introducing new talent, ranging from blues and jazz to soul and R&B, but there's always at least one night a week dedicated purely to jazz – check the Facebook page to find out which. To make a night of it, start with a dinner reservation on the top floor, an impressive colonial-inspired salon; the cuisine is Asian fusion and the cocktails are just right. If you want a front-row seat for the basement jazz, you can also reserve a dinner table front of house or just wander down after dessert.

(*50 rue de Charenton, 12ème; +33 1 43 46 08 09; open every day for lunch & dinner; Facebook.com/lechinaofficiel*)

Paris Jazz Corner

Cool cats, reminisce over this

Monday nights at **Le Piano Vache** bring you back to Paris in the late 1960s, when the student revolution was brewing in the *Quartier Latin*. The rotating resident musicians, reminiscent of Django Reinhardt, serenade the dedicated Parisian audience into the night with gypsy jazz. The warm red glow, the tattered music posters that make up the wallpaper, the dusty top-shelf bottles, rickety furniture – this old bar on a dimly lit backstreet is nothing short of a time warp. Johnny Depp was known to drop in and catch a gig here during his years as an American ex-pat.

(8 rue Laplace, 5ème; +33 1 46 33 75 03; lepianovache.fr; Mon-Sat)

Jazz Brunch Under the Olive Trees

Sunday brunch is a festive affair under the olive trees planted beneath the glass roof of **La Bellevilloise** in the bohemian 20th arrondissement, a historical workers' union turned restaurant, bar and cultural pop-up venue. It's become most famous for its weekly live jazz brunches, offering a cheery musical afternoon and a large buffet with pancakes piled high.

(19-21 rue Boyer, 20ème; +33 1 46 36 07 07; brunch seatings at 11.30am & 2pm)

Vinyl Collector

Crocojazz is a collector's den located in the heart of the city's historical jazz neighbourhood and should be an essential destination for any self-respecting devotee of the genre. There you'll meet Gilles, who speaks perfect English and has an encyclopaedic knowledge of jazz records. Be prepared to walk out with a renewed passion for vinyl collecting.

(64 rue de la Montagne Sainte Geneviève, 5ème; +33 1 46 34 78 38; Tues-Sat, 11am-7pm)

Phonogalerie

Behind a beautiful blue boutique façade, **Paris Jazz Corner** has a diverse collection of stuff you'd never find on iTunes: blues, bebop, soul, Latin American, world fusion and rare movie soundtracks from the '60s. Once you're done digging for vinyl, it's probably worth poking your head into the gardens just across the street, where you'll discover a Roman gladiator's amphitheatre, unearthed in the nineteenth century, smack in the middle of the city. No biggie. (*5 rue de Navarre, 5ème; parisjazzcorner.com Tues-Sat, 12-8pm*)

A few chapters back, I mentioned the Phono Museum (pg. 73) which is attached to a significant record store at the back, filled with rare recordings, antique gramophones and stunning original posters for sale. Jalal, the owner of **Phonogalerie**, has some serious poster art hanging in his shop, all professionally restored from the golden age of jazz. His collection of phonograph cylinders (the earliest commercial medium for recording and reproducing sound) is nothing to sniff at either. (*10 rue Lallier; 9ème; +33 1 45 26 45 80; open Thurs-Sat, 2pm-8pm, or you can book a private appointment*)

Just the Girls

My Secret Paris Girls' Lunch
Tell her to meet you at the prettiest flower shop in Paris at No. 14 *rue des Saint-Pères* and wait by the tulips stacked on top of old books. Next door is one of the city's oldest tabac shops, where you can stock up on glossy magazines to pore over during lunch together. Duck into No. 16 and follow the passageway all the way to the end, past the antique shops, until you reach the white French

13- A Baker's Dozen

doors with vines curling around the shopfront of **13- a Baker's Dozen**. Give in to the warm glow and the scent of pies baking in the oven that wrap around you like a warm blanket. Before you can even close the door behind you, a cheerful voice with a hint of a southern accent calls out to you as if you were old friends: 'Hey there!'

The chef and owner is Laurel Sanderson, an American domestic goddess living in Paris. She first came here for a three-day vacation nearly twenty years ago and she never went home. Laurel's been conjuring up recipes and memories from her native South Carolina mixed with local French ingredients ever since. Recipe books are stacked high on every available shelf and bowls full of fresh eggs sit on the counter waiting to be cracked into a cake mix. The menu, clipped onto a madeleine baking tray, reads like a ladies' lazy luncheon dream. You've got your naughty-but-nice Franco-American inspired options or some lighter choices for the *Parisienne* diet. If it's Mac 'n' Cheese Friday, take my word for it and treat yourself to a starter of the homemade good stuff. If you want some tips on how to make a few of Laurel's home-style recipes (along with some good company and a few glasses of wine), she hosts cooking classes that you can sign up for through the Facebook page (*facebook.com/treizeis13isthirteen*). You can also take one of the bag-painting workshops that are held here by one of Laurel's ex-pat designer friends (*kasiadietzworkshops.com*). It's the perfect start to a girls' weekend in Paris.

(*16 rue des Saints Pères, 7ème; +33 1 73 77 27 89; Tues-Sat, 10am-6pm*)

Supermom

If she stayed up late to finish all your costumes for school plays, sewed back on every lost button, or helped you pick out the perfect fabric for your first pair of drapes, my guess is Mama might enjoy a visit to the **Marché Saint-Pierre**. A step back in time, this fabric market has existed for sixty years and the whole block has since sprouted little havens for DIY style needs. Just across the road, **Reine** also has an impressive selection over several floors, where you can find exotic fabrics and accessories. Pick up some Liberty-print elbow pads to spruce up a winter sweater or add some rare buttons to that old coat of yours.

(*2 rue Charles Nodier, 18ème; marchesaintpierre.com; open Mon-Sat, 10am-6.30pm*)

*See Chapter 5's 'Shopping like a Parisian' for more retail therapy tips (pg. 106).

Fairy-Tale Montmartre

If you want to show her the real charms of Montmartre without bumping into busloads of tourists, start on *avenue Junot*, a wide cobblestone residential road that winds up the hill, lined with some of the most delicious architecture in Paris. The art deco ironwork, those tall glass artists' windows bathed in light, colourful cul-de-sacs peeking out at you from behind corners; here is the

Montmartre they wrote books and poems and made movies about. Ring the bell of the gate at No. 23 to visit the beautiful **Hôtel Particulier de Montmartre** and order a morning cup of tea in their garden (or in the covered winter garden if it's chilly). On the way out, poke your head into the courtyard on the right just before the gate leading back out to the street. The local pétanque club meets regularly here and might let you stick around if you flash a smile.

Stop for an organic lunch next door at **Marcel**, a trendy and reliable spot any day of the week. For the weekend brunch you'll find everything from Irish porridge to kale salads, but you'd be wise to book a table.
(*1 Villa Léandre, 18ème; +33 1 46 06 04 04; restaurantmarcel.fr; open every day, 11am–7pm & until 11pm on weekends*)

Charm your lunch date with a stroll down the **Villa Leandre**, the cobblestone pedestrian cul-de-sac just next to Marcel. You'll be admiring some of the most sought-after real estate in Paris; rows of unusual colourful cottages with peaked roofs. On the opposite sidewalk of *avenue Junot*, head into the *rue Simon-Dereure*. It looks like a dead end, but that's only for cars. There's a hidden garden to discover on your right, and if you take the elegant stone staircase at the end of the cul-de-sac, it will lead you up to the fairy-tale **Allée des Brouillards**. Spot the Sacré-Cœur towers in the distance. You're now on track for a scenic route to the top of the hill.

A Parisienne Chic Dinner

Les Chouettes is ideal for a celebratory reunion lunch or dinner with the girls. Layered on three levels of gorgeous art deco style, ask to start with a drink on the top floor, find a nook, order wine and admire the bird's-eye view of those monochrome floor tiles below. The menu is rather small (available in English) but it's made up for by the fact that each dish is very high quality and beautifully presented.

(*32 rue Picardie, 3ème; +33 1 44 61 73 21; restaurant-les-chouettes-paris.fr; open every day, 12pm-2am*)

Granny's Pantry

To wind down from a shopping spree at the famous Parisian department store Le Bon Marché, I recommend a tea break at **Mamie Gateaux**. The space is quaint, countrified and cosy like a French grandmother's kitchen, and the scones are crumbly, warm and buttery.

(*66 rue du Cherche-Midi, 6ème; mamie-gateaux.com; Tues-Sat, 11.45am-6pm*)

Previous: Hôtel Particulier de Montmartre

Above left: Les Chouettes

Right: Le Grand Colbert

Introducing your French Squeeze

Restaurant requirements: 1) polite waiters who aren't going to be rude to your English-speaking parents; 2) comfortable and not too loud, so they can understand your new amour's thick French accent; 3) somewhere that feels a little bit special.

Best Roast Chicken in Town

In case you were looking for it, the best *poulet rôti* in Paris is, without a doubt, at chez **Le Coq Rico**, a smart-casual Parisian eatery serving gourmet chicken in a picturesque backstreet of Montmartre, just behind the Sacré-Cœur. The concept of a chicken-only menu might sound odd, but let them surprise you with all the creative variations they've got up their sleeve. Mama's roast suddenly becomes 'special occasion' food that will impress even the most gourmand of foodies.

(*98 rue Lepic, 18ème; +33 1 42 59 82 89; en.lecoqrico.com; open every day for lunch & dinner*)

Not Old, a Classic

Earn extra points with Mom and Pop for taking them to **Le Grand Colbert**, the classic restaurant from that loveable movie with Jack Nicholson and Diane Keaton, *Something's Gotta Give*. A Parisian institution (a listed building, in fact), the food and service are both reliably good, so you won't have to worry about anything other than the conversation. And if it goes well with the parents, hopefully you won't have to worry about picking up the cheque either.

(*2 rue Vivienne, 2ème; +33 1 42 86 87 88; legrandcolbert.fr; open for lunch & dinner every day*)

Keep it Casual

For something lighter on Dad's pocket, **L'Ebauchoir** is a little-known place to wow the family with a totally unfussy yet delicious market-fresh meal. It's got that cool, laid-back east Paris vibe while also being very parent-friendly. The staff are happy people, there's a great bar and there's sidewalk seating for the warmer months. A very safe bet.

(*43- 45 rue de Cîteaux, 12ème; +33 1 43 42 49 31; lebauchoir.com; open Mon-Sat*)

Left: Vintage found photo

Opposite: Art et Metiers

The Kids are Coming Too

A Belle Époque Fairground

The **Musée des Arts Forains** is the result of one man's fascination with rare funfair objects, games, toys, theatrical props and other lost treasures dating back to the 1800s. At the heart of a neighbourhood in Paris that was once the main hub of wine bottling for the city, this magical museum is set in the nineteenth-century wine storehouses, where old train tracks still run through the cobblestoned streets in between the pavilions. Crystal chandeliers hang from the trees and there's a century-old carousel to be ridden. Take a magical trip through the charming history of playful treasures and be transported back to your childhood, when nothing was more important than playtime.
(*53 avenue des Terroirs de France, 12ème; visits must be reserved online at arts-forains.com*)

Around the World in 80 Minutes

Tell the kids you're taking them to see the original Batmobile, which is hanging from the ceiling of the **Museum of Arts et Métiers**. You'll have just as much fun as them, stepping into this world of Jules Verne-era industrial design. A seriously underrated museum that should be on more must-see lists.
(*60 rue Réaumur, 3ème; arts-et-metiers.net ; Tues- Sun, 10am-6pm, & Thurs until 9.30pm*)

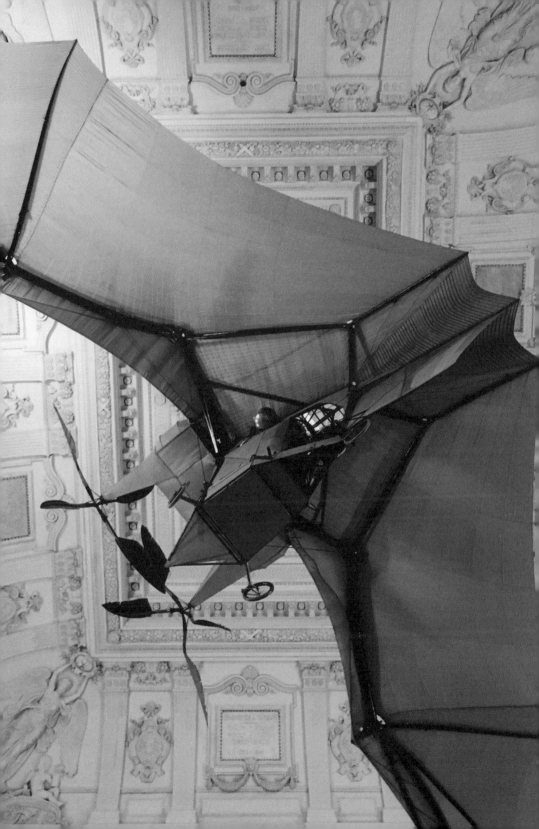

The Parisian Life Aquatic

Watch their faces light up when you tell them they can be the co-captain of their very own boat on the canals of Paris – no licence needed. Forget those big tourist boats that ferry up and down the Seine, barking the names of famous monuments at you over the loudspeaker. **Rent your own electric boat** for up to five people from €40 an hour, or one for seven people for the entire day at €28 a head. They'll even prepare a picnic basket for you on request. There are boats to accommodate up to eleven people and the same company also rents out badminton, pétanques and Mölkky sets to play along the canal.
(*Bassin de la Villette, 37 quai de la Seine, 19ème; find the details at boating-paris-marindeaudouce.com; open every day, 9.30am-10pm*)

The Time-Machine Sweet Shop

You could stand in the endless line at Ladurée, queuing up with the other macaron zombies, or you could go on a little hunt for someplace slightly more worth your precious time in Paris. **Le Bonbon Au Palais** is a unique sweet shop elaborately decorated to look like a charming 1950s French schoolroom; a pastel-coloured time machine to childhood. From platters of exotic candied fruits to jars filled with *guimauve* (old-fashioned marshmallows), Le Bonbon au Palais stocks some of the rarest candies in the world. Georges, the owner with the warm smile and an incurable passion for confectionery, literally curates his candy from small towns all across France. His sweets are so rare that each candy has its own patent from the age-old artisanal houses that are still producing them in the same little villages where they were first concocted. These patents protect the sweets from big confectionery companies copying their recipe or shape. Some houses even deliberately add various secret 'flaws' – specs of floral extract embedded in the candy to prove authenticity. Ask Georges to show you some.
(*19 rue Monge, 5ème; bonbonsaupalais.fr; Tues-Sat, 10.30am-7.30pm*)

Step Inside a Kaleidoscope

The *Palais des Mirages* (Hall of Mirrors) is no doubt the most unusual room in the city to step foot inside. The magnificent exhibition inside the **Musée Grevin** has been on show for well over a century, ever since it was created for the Paris Universal Exhibition in 1900. In addition to this kaleidoscopic wonderland, a visit to the historic waxwork museum includes ghoulish scenes from the French Revolution and a baroque magic show theatre.
(*10 boulevard Montmartre; 9ème; grevin-paris.com; open every day*)

Poirot's Mystery Train Dinner

Turn mealtime into an Agatha Christie novel at the **Victoria Station-Wagon Restaurant**; seated inside the cinematic velvet dining carriage of what could be an *Orient Express* train, you can imagine Poirot arriving on the scene ready

Place Dauphine

to solve one of his mysterious murder cases. Don't expect the food (Italian) to change your life, but I go for the indulgent pizzas and the feeling of travelling (both physically and through time) on a train that's never leaving Paris. Inspect your train carriage first on the hidden *Passage des Panoramas* before boarding at the main entrance.

(*11 boulevard Montmartre, 2ème; +33 1 42 36 73 90; open daily for lunch & dinner*)

Pétanque and Provence in Paris

Gather the family on the ***Place Dauphine***, with its picture-perfect cafés and sandy white terrain. This peaceful island enclave in the middle of the river Seine is the ideal spot for a hearty game of pétanque. No balls? Or *boules*, should I say? No problem. At the tip of the place, near the entrance, look for **Ma Salle à Manger**, the blue café with a red umbrella (*26 Place Dauphine*). They'll kindly lend you your very own pétanque set in return for buying a drink or a plate of cheese. Refreshments covered, claim a bench and play ball!

(*Place Dauphine, Île de la Cité, 1er; masalleamanger.fr*)

My Secret Paris Toyshop

In between the shopping boutiques on the *rue de Charonne*, you'll notice an open cobblestone passageway at No. 26. All along the leafy *Passage L'homme*, shells of former workshops and their weathered doorways line the cobbled path, some as old as the French Revolution. The sound of blacksmiths, cobblers and woodworkers hammering away with their instruments would have once filled this courtyard. We're here to see the toyshop, an old wooden storefront framed by overgrown vines, promising an enchanting world inside. Tin Tin books, toy cars and building blocks cheerfully fill the windows of **Librairie de la Bande Desinée**; part library of whimsical children's classics, part toyshop of handmade artisanal novelties. There's also a large comic-book store through a doorway at the back – a bit of a legendary collector's temple in Paris. Just another reason to always poke your head into Paris's cracks and crevices, leaving no door or passageway unexplored.

(*Passage l'Homme, 11ème; Mon-Sat, 10.30am-7.30pm*)

Crêpes, Toy Boats and Puppets in the Park

In the 1920s, a craftsman of miniature sailboats, Clement Paudeau, had the idea of renting out his model boats to children to sail on the *Grand Basin* of the Jardin du Luxembourg for two pennies a turn. With his wife by his side, Clement ran the little business by the pond known as **Les Voilliers du Luxembourg** for decades. Still to this day (weather permitting), the same colourful boats he painted almost one hundred years ago are wheeled out on a cart by his successor. The boats have now been assigned UNESCO Heritage status. It's hard to tell who's happier to see them set sail – the children or the nostalgic parents watching their kids gently pushing out their little yachts, hoping for a steady wind, guiding them with batons.

(*Le bassin du Jardin du Luxembourg; open Wed, 1pm-6pm; weekends & school holidays, 11am-6pm; €2 per boat*)

Librairie de la Bande
Desinée, Passage l'Homme

After a morning adventure on the high seas of the Jardin du Luxembourg, the sailors will need to be fed. South-west of the main pond, to the left of a statue of Queen Marie de Medicis, look for **Kiosque 7**, a small crêperie hut with handwritten menu boards. From a tiny bird's-nest kitchen, this charming food vendor will whip up a round of buttery crêpes with the freshest ingredients, as well as salads, tartines and ice cream to satisfy a hungry crew (and a pitcher of hot wine for the captain). After lunch, follow the park signposts to the **Marionnettes du Jardin du Luxembourg**, a puppet theatre that has been going strong since the 1930s.

(Shows start from 3pm, 4pm and there's a matinee at 11am; marionnettesduluxembourg.fr, €6 a head)

Family-Friendly Tables

- **Alma the Chimney Cake Factory**: You might have heard of funnel cakes before, a Romanian and Hungarian street food favourite that resembles a smoking chimney. Made of a raised (yeasted) dough, twisted around a stick and butter-basted while roasting on a spit, you can opt for the traditional sweet variations, but the sumptuous smell of the savory will win you over to stay for a full meal. The kids will appreciate the treehouse seating arrangements almost as much as you will.
  (59 boulevard Beaumarchais, 3ème; open Tues-Sun, 12pm-6pm)
- **Eggs & Co.**: Brunch in a country barn house, haystacks included.
  (11 rue Bernard Palissy, 6ème; +33 1 4544 02 52; open every day for lunch)
- **A Noste**: A trendy, modern, street-food inspired spot near Opéra that will cheer up even the moodiest of teenagers. High tables not ideal for very small children.
  (6 bis rue du 4 Septembre, 2ème; +33 1 47 03 91 91; open every day for lunch & dinner)
- **Bol Porridge Bar**: You never knew porridge could taste this good. This trendy little café takes the kids' breakfast staple to a whole new level of sweet and savoury gastronomy.
  (76 Rue du Faubourg Poissonnière, 10ème; bolporridgebar.com; open Mon-Sat for breakfast & lunch)
- **Ma Cocotte**: On a family outing to the Paris flea market, where steak tartare, frogs' legs and snails might seem like the only thing on offer, opt for the easy menu of Philippe Starck's restaurant; a spacious and stylish market oasis.
  (106 rue des Rosiers, Saint-Ouen; +33 1 49 51 70 00; macocotte-lespuces.com; open every day for lunch & dinner)
- **Jeanne B**: A chic but laid-back ambience with fresh country-kitchen dishes you would usually have to take a three-hour train down south for.
  (61 rue Lepic, 18ème or 42 rue Jean-Pierre Timbaud, 11ème; +33 1 42 51 17 53; open every day, 10am-10.30pm)

*Need an English-speaking babysitter? baby-speaking.fr/en

Greatest Hits

How to do Versailles with everyone smiling in the family photo...
If you're going to do Versailles – and I know this might sound odd – I
recommend skipping the tour inside the main palace. It's far too crowded with
tourists holding selfie sticks and there's nothing enjoyable about sharing an
experience with that many iPhone screens. Head straight to Marie Antoinette's
'smaller' chateau on the grounds, **Le Petit Trianon**. On her side of the park,
you'll find all the charming follies she had built in her Trianon garden, including
a fake peasant hamlet, her own personal theatre, and several miniature
pavilions for entertaining. Also keep an eye out for the tiny vineyard hidden
in the park. After a long day, treat yourselves to some fancy cocktails at the
Gordon Ramsay bar in the **Trianon Palace Hotel**.
(*1 boulevard de la Reine, 78000 Versailles*)

Iconic Tables
Launched by an ambitious French waiter who went into business with a
beautiful courtesan, **Maxim's** is a Parisian legend; *the* symbol of art nouveau
decadence. Founded in 1893, its customers over the years have included Marcel
Proust, Maria Callas, Brigitte Bardot, John Travolta and Lady Gaga. Book a
table for lunch and enquire about the English-language tour of the little-known
museum upstairs at 2pm. Three floors of art nouveau objects, furnishings and
fashion await in the **Musee 1900**.
(*3 rue Royale, 8ème; +331 4265 27 94; musee1900.com; both restaurant & museum
open Wed-Sat*)

Harry's Bar in Paris is the original Harry's Bar and the alleged birthplace of
the Bloody Mary. A small corner of Manhattan – quite literally – in the heart of
Paris, the founder actually dismantled the bar of a New York saloon and had
it shipped here. The walls are covered with relics dedicated to the American
in Paris, from handwritten notes to pennants of American colleges. Since 1911,
the restaurant/pub has attracted ex-pats, writers, musicians and movie stars,
including Hemingway, Sartre, Fitzgerald, Gershwin and Bogart. Even James Bond
called it the best place in Paris to get a 'solid drink'. In Ian Fleming's short story
'From a View to a Kill', Bond recalls following the directions to Harry's Bar from a
newspaper advertisement in his youth, 'Just tell the taxi driver: *Sank Roo Doe Noo.*'
(*5 rue Daunou, 2ème; +331 42 61 71 14; open every day for lunch & dinner, 12pm-2am*)

La Coupole was the party temple of the roaring twenties, where the likes of Man
Ray, Picasso, Josephine Baker and Hemingway sat elbow to elbow. Today it's
still an art deco paradise and remains one of the truly classic brasseries in Paris.
(*102 boulevard du Montparnasse, 14ème; lacoupole-paris.com open every day.*)

Above: Inside the pavilions
of the gardens of Versailles
Overleaf: The nineteenth-
century Paris Morgue

And for the more unconventional family who delight in the macabre...

That time when Parisians used to hang out at the Morgue for fun

Every day, some thirty thousand people visit *Notre Dame de Paris*, but little known to tourists or even to the Parisians passing by on their daily commute, there was once a much more popular, yet sinister, attraction that shared a backyard with the historic cathedral. Capable of luring up to forty-thousand visitors in a single day, that attraction was the Paris Morgue.

There aren't many other ways to describe the Paris Morgue during the nineteenth century other than as a place of entertainment, for Parisians and tourists alike. The original purpose of the open morgue was not to attract tourism but to identify unknown bodies found in the city, urging friends and families to claim their deceased. Some had been fished out of the Seine, other were suicides that no one had reported missing. Their unfortunate remains were displayed on slanted marble tables behind glass, the victims' clothes and belongings hung on pegs behind them.

Word of the morbid (and free) exhibition of lifeless bodies quickly spread, and soon the morgue became a fixture on the Parisian social circuit, enticing the curiosity of men, women, even children from all social backgrounds, who would visit regularly. Filing eagerly past the grisly displays, they acquired at least a week's worth of fresh gossip on the possible identities of the corpses and their causes of death. Outside on the Quai de l'Archevêché, street vendors catered to the crowds that flocked to the morgue, peddling cookies, gingerbread, coconut slices and other touristy fairground treats of the era.

'There are few people having visited Paris who do not know the Morgue ... one of the most popular sights in Paris,' wrote Parisian social commentator Hughes Leroux in 1888. Charles Dickens was known to be a frequent visitor and describes the Paris Morgue in several of his journals as an 'old acquaintance', and 'a strange sight, which I have contemplated many a time during the last dozen years'. The identification of dead people was turned into circus entertainment, listed in practically every guidebook for the city. Today, in the exact spot where the Paris Morgue was located from 1867 to 1907, there stands a public garden, Square de l'Ile de France. It's right next to the most scenic photo opportunity in front of Notre Dame, where tourists take a romantic pause on the bridge, blissfully unaware of the dark history behind them.

Not far from this spot, the morbidity continues at a century-old little museum run by the French police, inside a police station. Two thousand unique objects evoke the history of crime in Paris, including glass-encased murder weapons with suspicious stains, a gruesome archive of police photography, and even skeletal remains. **Le musée de la préfecture de Police** is open every day from 9am-5pm.
(*4 rue de la Montagne Sainte-Geneviève, 5ème; +33 1 44 41 52 50*)

Les Frigos

08

Paris in Wonderland: Down the Rabbit Hole

Nessy,

Allow me to introduce myself. My name is Dora. I'm twenty-two years old and a little too adventurous for my own good, if there is such a thing. When I came across your article about disappearing down manholes into the Paris catacombs, I knew it was right up my alley. Some adventurers feel the best way to preserve the spirit that comes along with such a sport is by keeping secrets. Others feel the best way to keep the spirit alive is to share those secrets. I would like to determine which adventurer you are.

My partner and I are planning a trip to Paris (conveniently around Halloween), and we would like to have some illicit underground adventures to look forward to. Any help with this would be more than appreciated.

Dora
Sent from my prehistoric stone tablet

Did you know there's a library inside the Paris catacombs? It's not the kind of library that requires you to check out your books at the front desk or return them by a certain time. You'll need much more than a library card to access the city's buried bibliothèque.

Crouching over in metre-high pitch black passageways is not something you're ever quite prepared for – even with the promise of spectacular underground art or turquoise swimming pools. Going down into the catacombs, the real catacombs, is not a walk in the park. There is no easy access, no safety guaranteed and everything about it is illegal.

Only a tiny section is open to the public. The rest (some 300km of terrain) is claimed by a codified micro-community that calls itself 'the cataphiles'. They do not easily welcome first-timers to their underground sanctuary. It's a world they believe you need to work for; a privilege that can only come with patience and tenacity. You're in their underworld, and the rules are different in the darkness. A cataphile won't agree to be your guide because you send them a friendly email. You'll need to be introduced by someone they trust.

Yes, I do know a cataphile or two. I've followed them down manholes as bewildered Parisians drinking wine watched our heads disappearing one by one below the surface. I've wriggled through holes the size of a cat door to reach a vast gallery covered in murals and trudged through waist-deep water to find an underground beach. If you ask me what kind of adventurer I am, hands down, I'm the kind that wants to share my experiences. But some adventures hold more risk than others, so be careful what you ask for. From the risk-free to the risqué to the 'at your own risk', enjoy responsibly...

Abandoned & Underground

A Walk Along the Abandoned Inner-City Railway

Look for the painted zoo animals peeping over the brick wall on *rue Florian* where it meets *rue Galleron* (20ème), and a few metres further you'll find a graffiti-tagged gate that's usually – hopefully – unlocked. Your best chances are on a Sunday afternoon, when local urban gardeners tend to leave it open behind them. Proceed to tiptoe/skip/dance down the train tracks of **La Petite Ceinture**, a surviving relic of a bygone era. Built in 1862, closed since 1934, the railroad was a circular route (hence, 'the little belt'), connecting the main train stations of Paris within the old fortified city walls. When the métro was introduced, the little belt no longer had much of a purpose and the tracks were abandoned, left to grow wild, relinquished to the underworld. Today, this forgotten expressway is a neat way to see Paris from a different perspective, as the railroad's bridges peep over the boulevards every few hundred yards and the tracks run along the back of artist ateliers of the 20th arrondissement that you can't see from the street. Just remember where you entered from, and, unless you're well equipped, I'd recommend doing a U-turn when you encounter long dark tunnels. Post-stroll, grab a beer on the **Mama Shelter** terrace overlooking the railroad you were just exploring.

(*109 rue de Bagnolet, 20ème*)

La Petite Ceinture

The Clandestine Party Planners

So, there's planning a party and then there's planning a party in a secret abandoned location in Paris. A candlelit banquet in an abandoned chateau, a 1940s bash in a secret Cold War bomb shelter – does it sound up your alley? If you're interested in exploring the Paris catacombs or anything else truly underground in this city, I can only recommend that you become involved in the world of **We Are the Oracle**. A secretive group that surfaced in the French capital a few years ago, We Are the Oracle throw once-in-a-lifetime soirées for Parisians looking to party somewhere a little more off the grid. If you're wondering how to meet some of Paris's urban explorers and fellow enthusiasts of the underworld, this is how. The master of ceremonies – or as he might prefer to call himself, '*le conspirateur*' – has a knack for pinning down the most impossible locations you could imagine to host extravagant shindigs. This young sir has become a close confidante of mine over the years in Paris, so don't be shy about going over and introducing yourself as a friend of a friend (that's me). You can't miss him at one of his events, he goes by Foulques (pronounced 'Foolk') and usually makes a theatrical speech to kick off the evening.

Here's how to get invited: 1) join the Oracle's secret society (sign up to their newsletter); 2) wait for the newsletter to arrive in your inbox detailing the next event; 3) the secret location won't be revealed until the day of. Show up in the right gear for the evening's theme and prepare for a night to remember. The collective can also create your own private event. A tiny bit interested? It might be worth planning that little trip around one of their upcoming parties. And you can bet I'll be there too, lurking around in the shadows somewhere. (*Test the waters and stay updated via their Facebook page facebook.com/wearetheoracle*)

Right: Underground dinner parties with We Are the Oracle

Page 168: Private event space for hire in Les Frigos

Happy Hour in an Abandoned Métro Station

There's another layer to the American dive bar **L'Entre Potes** that many patrons are too busy enjoying the good whiskey and friendly ambience to ever discover. What lies beneath is the remains of an abandoned métro station, which the owner of the bar remarkably moved here to create a truly unique underground scene in his arched cellar. It looks like a bona fide ghost station turned speakeasy, complete with the iconic white tiled mosaics of the Parisian underground, métro signs and official panels. Ask Ali, the friendly owner, for the full story over a Long Island drink at the bar.

(14 rue de Charonne, 11ème; +33 1 48 06 57 04; open Tues-Sat, 6pm to 2am, or 4am on weekends, and the basement can be privatised upon request)

Dining in a Giant Abandoned Fridge

There's an enormous old building infamously claimed by squatters back in the 1980s standing defiantly in the middle of a modernised neighbourhood of the 13th arrondissement in Paris. Surrounded by contemporary glass apartment blocks, the building is covered in impressive street art and has a great big water tower that would make an ideal lookout for any fortress. It's known as **Les Frigos**, literally meaning 'the fridges', and once served as a refrigerated railway depot for storing food and produce headed for the city's markets. Essentially a giant refrigerator (which explains the water tower), it operated from the 1920s until the 1960s, when a number of artists began squatting in the industrial wasteland left behind. The building quickly became synonymous with art and rebellion while authorities grappled to expel the tenants. After many years fighting a losing battle to vacate the vagabonds, the city hall finally agreed to buy the building and ensure that the artists could stay and create with the law on their side. Having won the right to freely occupy the building, the residents formed an organisation under the adopted name of *Les Frigos*. Today over two hundred artists legally work and live in this multistorey building, and members are quick to point out that despite appearances, they are not squatters.

The inside of the Les Frigos is just as intriguing as the façade. Every stairwell, corridor and elevator shaft is covered in painted murals and you're welcome to wander in. There are some truly incredible artists' studios to discover behind closed doors, however these are open to the public only on special visitor or exhibition days, or by private appointment. (*Les-frigos.com*)

To get a sense of the community here, you can also have lunch at one of the site's unlikely restaurants. Tucked away at the back of the building is **La Maison des Frigos**, the best-kept secret café of the artists in residence. Simple and fresh bento is prepared from a seasonal market menu by the friendly Japanese owner, Mariko.

(19 rue des Frigos, 13ème; +33 1 44 23 76 20; Mon-Fri)

Even more secret is **The Office**, a gourmet supper club run by Emilie, 'a child of the refrigerators', who grew up inside these graffiti-covered walls, playing in the old elevators and hanging around the workshops with her bohemian parents. When Emilie grew up, she decided she was going to become a chef, and so in the newsroom of an indie magazine which operates out of Les Frigos, when all the journalists have gone home, she begins setting up her clandestine restaurant. Emilie graduated from one of France's leading culinary schools, so you can expect a truly gourmet meal in the unlikeliest of settings. The Office caters for an open table of up to twelve guests. You can either reserve a seat amongst new friends for €40 a head or privatise the whole table for your entourage. (*Reservations at theofficelatable.com*)

Emilie is not the only resident of Les Frigos willing to throw a party in this historic location. Hidden behind a graffiti-covered metal door on the third floor, Italian artist-in-residence Paolo Calia created his very own red velvet 'Liberace' palace of kitsch that can be hired for special events and private celebrations. It can be your candlelit wonderland too, for an evening – as long as you remember to drop me an invitation.
(*Les-frigos.com*)

The Art of Squatting

I first met one of the founders of **Madame Lupin** in the Paris catacombs on Halloween one year, sharing a bottle of red wine, crouching on some ancient limestone. He told me about the secret gourmet picnics he liked to organise in abandoned chateaux around the city's suburbs. Then one day he fell in love with a girl who worked in a big Parisian art gallery and the two decided to combine his little black book of hidden hideouts with her curator's eye. Together they became Madame Lupin, a clandestine hostess of the Parisian underworld for gastronomy and the arts. Past events include a stunning exhibition in an underground sand cave. Another saw the eleventh floor of an abandoned museum transformed into a giant canvas for a sculptor who covered an entire wall in shark eggshells. Madame Lupin works tirelessly to find new painters, sculptors, performers, musicians and patrons of the arts to be a part of her story.

(*See Madamelupin.com or facebook.com/lesvernissagesdemadamelupin*)

Art 'squats' are in fact a key part of Parisian history and its bohemian culture. Picasso's Bateau-Lavoir, the infamous artists' residence in Montmartre where he first discussed Cubism and painted 'Les Desmoiselles d'Avignon' was, indeed, a squat. Where would the art world be if Paris had not become Picasso's patron at a time when he was burning his own drawings to keep his fire lit in the winter?

As it turns out, art 'squats', legalised and yet-to-be-legalised, can be found all over town. Take **59 Rivoli** on one of the city centre's busiest boulevards, where in the late '90s over thirty artists moved into a grand Haussmann-era building previously owned by the Credit Lyonnais bank. The artists began decorating the façade with their avant-garde art, causing a bit of a stir and attracting quite the crowd. Today it's a legitimate studio space for artists, also known as the 'Aftersquat'.

(*59 rue de Rivoli, 1er, Tues- Sun, 1pm-8pm*)

Following the example of 59 Rivoli, several more abandoned and squatted spaces were bought by the city hall and renovated as legitimate workshops. Squatting artists were allowed to stay in residence for as little as €1 a day on the condition that they continued to produce their work and give the public access to see it.

The **Point Éphémère**, a former factory on the Canal Saint-Martin and today a trendy café, bar, exhibition space and concert venue, also started out as a squat in the '80s.

(*200 Quai de Valmy, 10ème; pointephemere.org; open every day, 12.30pm till late*)

The Haunting Human Zoo of Paris

In the furthest corner of the Vincennes woods of Paris lie the remains of what was once a public exhibition to promote French colonialism. Established over one hundred years ago, it was what we can only refer to today as the equivalent of a human zoo. In 1907, six different villages were built in the **Jardin d'Agronomie Tropicale**, representing all the corners of the French colonial empire at the time: Madagascar, Indochine, Sudan, Congo, Tunisia and Morocco.

The villages and their pavilions were built to recreate the life and culture of these countries; this included mimicking the architecture, importing the agriculture and, appallingly, inhabiting the replica houses with people who were brought to Paris from the faraway territories. The human inhabitants of the 'exhibition' were observed by over 1 million curious visitors from May until October 1907. (*It's estimated that from the 1870s until the 1930s, more than 1.5 billion people visited various exhibits around the world featuring human inhabitants.*)

Today, the Jardin d'Agronomie Tropicale is treated as a stain on France's history. Kept out of sight behind rusty padlocked gates for most of the twentieth century, the pavilions are decaying and the rare 'exotic' plantations have long disappeared. In 2006, the public was once again granted access to the gardens, but few people actually come to visit at all.

The entrance is marked by a 10ft Asian-inspired portico of rotting wood and faded red paint that stands like the ghost of a slain gatekeeper. Upon entering, you can instantly sense that this is not a place of which the French are proud. During the high noon of Imperialist Europe, spectators gawked at bare-breasted African women and were entertained by re-enactments of 'primitive life' in the colonies. Here, anthropologists and researchers could observe whole villages of tribespeople and gather physical evidence for their theories on racial superiority. The distinction between person and specimen was blurred. They were not guests here. They were nameless faces on the other side of a barrier. A hundred years on and there's still an eerie sense of ladies clutching sun parasols and men in bowler hats arriving, eager to see the show on the other side of this now crumbling colonnade. Now, nature has overtaken the pathways that lead to the various neglected monuments and condemned houses.

There are rumours that one building, the Indochine pavilion, might be refurbished to function as a small museum and research centre. It may be an intelligent solution to a delicate subject. If the French government destroyed the garden there could be accusations of attempting cover up the past. And so it remains, hauntingly beautiful; a neglected embarrassment. Tropical plants plucked from their homelands have been left to mutate in a junkyard of French colonial history.

(*Jardin d'Agronomie Tropicale, 45 bis avenue de la Belle Gabrielle, 75012 Paris. RER station: Nogent-sur-Marne; open every day, 9.30am-8pm*)

Jardin d'Agronomie Tropicale

The Rotting Rothschild Mansion

The Rothschilds are known as one of the greatest European banking dynasties ever established, amassing the largest private fortune in modern history. The family is less well known for anything to do with squalor, ruin or decay. But five miles from Notre Dame, beyond the lush green lawn of the Edmond-de-Rothschild Park, standing defiantly behind a thick wall of shrubbery and bramble is the ghostly figure of the **Chateau Rothschild**. The neo-Louis XIV castle has been abandoned since World War II, when the Rothschild family fled to England before the arrival of the Germans, who would later inhabit and plunder the house during the four-year Nazi occupation of Paris. After the city's liberation, soldiers of the U.S. Army were the next self-service tenants at the Chateau Rothschild, and their stay didn't do the residence any favours either. The Rothschilds never returned to their home in western Paris and over the decades it has been left to deteriorate, while serving as a playground for graffiti artists and vandals.

This once grand house was owned by one of the richest men in the world in the early nineteenth century, James Mayer de Rothschild, whose personal fortune (not including his family's) is thought to have been at least five times the fortune accumulated by Bill Gates. James and his wife Betty hosted the most lavish parties of the epoch within these walls. As major art patrons of the time, their guest list regularly included the likes of Rossini, Chopin, Balzac and Delacroix, as well as a who's who of the financial, entrepreneurial and political worlds.

As the clinking of champagne glasses, laughter and music rang through the halls, it would have been unimaginable to think that the Chateau de Rothschild would one day find itself in this sorry state. In the late 1970s, the Rothschild family sold the estate back to the city for a symbolic 1 franc. It was then very quickly sold off to a wealthy Saudi Arabian buyer for 50 million francs

Chateau Rothschild

(something close to €7 million today). Three decades later, under the same ownership, the historical monument is still in ruins, with an estimated €30 million bill for the renovation. The park remains open to the public and we can now picnic on the lawn with a front-row seat to this spectacular abandoned ruin – that is, if it doesn't turn one's stomach off the cheese and crackers. There are no guided tours for this historical monument, although my elusive friends at We are the Oracle (pg. 166) did hold a clandestine candlelit banquet here once. Of course I must stress that despite the measly fence surrounding the property, the chateau itself is not open to visitors, even if the graffiti suggests otherwise. (*Find the entrance to the park at 3 rue des victoires, Boulogne–Billancourt, Hauts de Seine; just a hop over the road from the south-east entrance of Bois de Boulogne; open 9am-5.30pm in winter & till 8pm in summer*)

A Suburban Paris Ghost Town

A thirty-minute drive north from central Paris lies a ghost town where very little has changed since the mid-twentieth century – except for one deafening adjustment. In the 1970s, the fate of this peaceful farming village changed drastically when the residents of **Goussainville-Vieux Pays** suddenly found themselves living under the direct flightpath of the country's largest airport. The low-flying air traffic going in and out of the newly built Charles de Gaulle Airport quickly became unbearable to live with and residents of the old village began deserting their homes in droves.

Goussainville-Vieux Pays

Today, at the heart of the village, is the skeleton of a once grand nineteenth-century bourgeois chateau. It appears to have been the victim of a fire that claimed the roof, leaving the interior, with its ornate frescoes, to the elements. The lawn seems like the perfect place for a midsummer picnic – and then the thundering engines of a Boeing 747 shatter the peace. Built in 1860 by the town's wealthiest family (whose descendants still own it), my guess is they would have been among first to abandon their home in Goussainville, unable to tolerate the noise of jumbo jets flying overhead and disturbing their garden parties.

In the summer of 1973, during the Salon de Bourget air show that was taking place in the proximity of the new Charles de Gaulle airport, a Soviet prototype plane designed to compete with the Concorde crashed in Goussainville, destroying several houses and a children's school that was luckily closed on that day. All six passengers on the plane and eight people on the ground perished. You could say that was more or less the final nail in the coffin for Goussainville.

Responsible for the abandonment of almost 150 properties in the village, the airport authorities were forced by decree to buy the abandoned houses and look after them. Of the 144 houses, the airport acquired 80. You'll find most of their doors and windows walled up, like silenced witnesses to a crime. Goussainville's renaissance church, Saint-Pierre-Saint-Paul is ranked as an historic monument, along with all of the buildings within its perimeter, eliminating the cost-effective option to simply demolish them (which would have been the airport's preferred solution). Instead, they had them sealed up and, despite the agreement, left them to decay. Only in 2010, after *Aéroports de Paris* sold half of the village back to the community for a symbolic price of €1, did local authorities finally step in and begin efforts to restore the fourteenth-century Renaissance church, which had suffered years of neglect. But still the jets roar overhead.

Only a handful of faithful villagers remain in Goussainville-Vieux Pays. Most residents were relocated to a brand new town several kilometres to the north. Frozen in time, the only presence that still breathes life into the old village is the improbable **Librairie Goussainlivres**, a labyrinthine that has managed to stay afloat in the ghost town for over twenty years since it opened in 1997. Filled with second-hand rarities, here you'll find Nicolas, the friendly bookseller who offers a warm welcome in contrast to the surreal uninhabited silence of the village outside.

(14 Place Hyancinthe Drujon, 95190 Goussainville, Le 'Vieux-Pays'; +33 1 39 88 29 09; open Tues-Sat, 11am-5pm, closed in Feb & Aug)

Exploring the Parisian Sewers

Forget boat rides down the Seine, if you were a tourist in Paris in the nineteenth and early twentieth century, the subterranean sewers were the hot ticket. In an 1869 travel guide to the City of Light 'for the English and American Traveller', Paris's new state-of-the-art sewer system came highly recommended.

At the height of the Belle Époque, Paris had come to possess one of the most comprehensive and efficient systems in Europe. The city, founded on the site of an early Roman city called Lutéce, had once relied on natural streams to wash away the waste. As the population grew, chamber pots were emptied into the streets, and later cesspits and cesspools were used. For a very long time, Paris was, in short, a stinky mess.

The 1840s-1890s saw the construction of '*Les Egouts*', a complex system of over 500 kilometres of sewers under Paris. By 1930, each street in the once putrid city had its very own sewer. It was the pride of Paris - so much so that they turned it into a tourist attraction.

'Sewerman' became a legal profession and tours were given by these sewermen on weekends. Surreal illustrations and photographs from the era show tourists, ladies included, wearing their Sunday best on boat rides through the sewage systems of Paris as if it were a Disneyland attraction. The boat tours were eventually scrapped, but the museum of **Les Egouts de Paris** is still a thing, and travellers looking to discover the underbelly, or should I say, the bowels of picturesque Paris can visit the sewers from Saturday to Wednesday for €3.50. While you might be thinking the city would need to pay you to visit, the museum does take visitors through some rather impressive tunnels in the system and you'll find Napoleon's seal inscribed on many of the walls. Its entrance is just a few minutes' walk from the Eiffel Tower.

(*Pont de l'Alma, place de la Resistance, opposite 93 quai d'Orsay, 7ème; egouts. tenebres.eu; open every day except Thurs & Fri, 11am-4pm, and 5pm in summer*)

Unmasking the Parisian Phantom of the Opera

What if I told you there is a lake under the Paris Opera House that is believed to be the very lake they speak of in *The Phantom of the Opera*? Underneath the iconic **Opéra Garnier**, in a dingy room with a square-shaped hole in the middle of the floor, rests a ladder that descends into the darkness.

It was in this very building, under the sprawling staircases and hidden doors of the baroque opera house, that the famous haunting fable written by Gaston Leroux was conceived. Originally published in a newspaper in 1909, the story begins: 'The Phantom of the Opera did exist.' Leroux's novel is saturated with people that really lived, events that actually happened and places you can still visit today, including the phantom's elusive lake.

The architect of the eponymous opera house, Charles Garnier, ran into a slight problem while digging its foundation. He had hit an arm of the Seine hidden below ground and no matter how hard his workers tried to pump out the water, it kept rushing back in. Rather than move location entirely, Garnier adjusted his drafts to control the water in cisterns, creating a sort of artificial subterranean lake. While it looks nothing like the famous romantic lagoon in the musical, the opera's staff enjoys feeding the resident fish and the Paris fire department

Cemetière de Montmartre

even goes diving there from time to time. As for those infamous rumours of a resident phantom? The Phantom of the Opera is there, at least inside my mind. (*Book a guided tour via www.cultival.fr/en*)

Occult Paris

The Misfit Mausoleums of Montmartre

At the foot of Montmartre, under a heavy wrought-iron bridge that skims the tops of blackened mausoleums, forgotten souls are spending their afterlives in perpetual darkness. Cemeteries are usually curious places to begin with, but the **Cemetière de Montmartre** is a very particular sort of misfit in the Parisian urban landscape.

Renowned local artists of Montmartre such as Degas are buried here, and many families of the nineteenth-century Parisian elite paid top dollar for prime plots near the entrance of the cemetery, where the sun would shine on the graves of their ancestors for centuries to come. Or so they thought.

Baron Haussmann, the man responsible for the transformation of Paris into the city we know today, had other ideas. As part of his urban planning that saw colossal avenues cut through the chaotic mass of small streets that made up Paris, he decided to build a road to Montmartre that would open it up to the west. It just so happened that his plan involved trampling all over quite a few graves.

As Haussmann commenced building his bridge and moving graves to make room for the giant iron pillars, the protests began, halting construction. The families whose graves would be disturbed by the bridge were offered new plots, free of charge, but the project was hotly debated in court. In the end, Haussmann managed to get his way and the bridge was finally built, leaving countless graves in the perpetual shadow of Parisian urbanisation.

Strangely enough, this outrageous lack of respect for the dead makes it one of the most fascinating cemeteries in the world. The clunky industrial blue iron bridge and the intricately carved stone mausoleums from another era are like mismatched puzzle pieces trying to fit together in this evolving city. Opposite symbols, past and future, tangled here together; Haussmann's error in judgement makes for beautiful irony. In our ever-changing urban landscapes, you have to wonder if something like this would be allowed to happen today. (*20 avenue Rachel, 18ème; open every day, 9am-6pm*)

The X-Rated Paris Grave

I see the **Père Lachaise Cemetery** as a miniature town of its own. The meandering pathways actually have their own official street names and signage, and the elaborate tombs look like rows of beautiful miniature gothic houses. Jim Morrison, Edith Piaf, Oscar Wilde, Frédéric Chopin, Maria Callas and Marcel Proust, to name a few, are all buried here. But there is one grave amongst the maze of tombs that's not quite like the others. And apparently this grave is very happy to see you.

Père Lachaise Cemetery

Victor Noir died under very unusual circumstances. He was a journalist in Paris when he became involved in an editorial dispute with a rival newspaper over a letter published by Prince Bonaparte. The details are a little hazy, but all you really need to know is that in 1870, Noir and his mates were challenged to a duel by Prince Bonaparte. Victor ended up getting slapped in the face by the Prince, and then shot dead. Almost 100,000 Parisians attended his funeral procession, outraged that the already unpopular Prince Bonaparte, great-nephew of Napoleon, was acquitted of the murder. A realistic life-sized bronze statue was sculpted to place above his tomb, portraying the slain journalist at the moment of his death as he fell backwards, dropping his top hat beside him.

For reasons unknown, the statue of Noir has a curiously noticeable bulge in his trousers. With the Père Lachaise Cemetery being the temple of superstition and Parisian folklore that it is, over the years Victor's grave became a symbol of fertility, especially amongst women. According to the myth, kissing the statue on the lips, rubbing its genital area and placing a flower in the upturned top hat will enhance fertility, bring a blissful sex life, or secure a husband within the year.

As a result of the legend (and many years of rubbing), the area around his genitals has become rather well worn and shiny in comparison to the rest of the grey-green oxidised bronze, leaving an unfortunate-looking stain on his trousers.

In 2004, a fence was built around the grave to prevent women from touching the statue and committing other inappropriate acts on a person's grave, but due to supposed protests from the 'female population of Paris', the fence was taken down and Victor now awaits your visit.

(*Track down the sexiest grave in Paris at 16 rue du Repos, 20ème; open every day, 9am-6pm*)

Scandalous Paris: Brothels & Bordellos of the Past

Tales of the Belle Époque Brothels

Behind No. 12 *rue Chabanais*, a typical building on a typical backstreet not far from the Louvre museum, used to be one of the most notorious and prestigious bordellos of the golden era. Today, it's your typical Haussmanian apartment building, but just across the road at No. 11, an inconspicuous little boutique gallery is keeping the sordid secrets of its lustful past alive.

Worlds apart from Paris's vast official art galleries and museums, **Au Bonheur du Jour** is run by a former cabaret dancer, Nicole Canet, who began compiling and selling old erotic photos at the Paris flea market after giving up her career as a performer, and today refers to herself as an 'archeologist of erotica'. From photographs, books and paintings to antique sex toys and original pieces of decor from the bordellos, Nicole is dedicated to uncovering the lost world of the '*maisons closes*' (brothels). 'Au Bonheur du Jour' in English means 'afternoon delight', alluding to the pleasures of stolen trysts.

Her unusual intimate gallery sits facing the old site of **Le Chabanais**, one of the most luxurious *maisons closes* in Paris during its heyday of authorised brothels. Adorned like a palace of pleasure to cater to any fantasy, Le Chabanais was no back-alley hotel; it was practically a national monument, listed as a site to see by the travel agencies of the era. The Prince of Wales (son of Queen Victoria) had his very own room at the establishment that carried his coat of arms above the bed. As a frequent visitor, the Prince, better known as 'Bertie', would bathe with Parisian prostitutes in a giant copper bath filled with champagne and enjoy threesomes in a lavish chair he called his 'love seat'. The copper bathtub, which was adorned with a half-woman-half-swan figurehead, was later bought by Salvador Dalí for 112,000 francs.

At Nicole's exhibitions you will always find fascinating items, such as an old wooden box fitted with a stereoscope lens that was used by male patrons to view pictures of the women on offer at the brothel, like a menu. The gallery often highlights the decor of the bordellos, with rare photographs of the elaborately themed rooms for which they were famous. Renowned painters even helped decorate the most palatial of the bordellos – the celebrated Belle Époque artist Henri Toulouse-Lautrec was commissioned to paint sixteen murals for the boudoirs in Le Chabanais. He was also a frequent patron. (*Au Bonheur du Jour: 1 rue Chabanais, 2ème; Tues-Sat, 2.30pm-7.30pm; keep track of new exhibitions at Aubonheurdujour.net*)

Twentieth-Century Bordello Hopping

When you're digging through Parisian flea markets or brocantes, keep your eye out for the much sought-after *Guide Rose*, the little black book of the Belle Époque; a pocket-sized Michelin-style guide to the pleasure establishments of Paris, the provinces and even France's foreign colonies. They are extremely rare and collectors daren't part with them, but one never knows what treasures can end up at the flea markets. A decadent journey through the Belle Époque brothels, the guide provided gentlemen with details on a venue's sexual specialities, its star courtesan and, importantly, its prices.

It would have listed, for example, the post-World War I brothel One-Two-Two, which opened in 1924 on *rue de Provence* and became the main competitor of Le Chabanais. Not as exclusively elitist, One-Two-Two was popular with soldiers and celebrities alike. On Thursday nights, the venue even held a special free night for wounded soldiers. Catering to all fetishes, each of the twenty-two rooms was inspired by a different time and place. A pirate room featured a mechanical boat swing and water jets that sprayed clients and courtesans as they did the dirty. An *Orient Express* room allowed customers to live out their sexual fantasies on a train inside a bouncing carriage with a railway soundtrack.

In its famous restaurant *Le Boeuf à la Ficelle*, waitresses served customers while dressed in nothing but their high heels. Cary Grant and Edith Piaf were patrons, and during the Nazi occupation the X-rated establishment was highly popular among the German officers. When the war ended, the French persecuted the courtesans of One-Two-Two and publicly shaved their heads.

Famed novelist Marcel Proust was a frequent patron of brothels and even joined other high-society figures in investing in two of Paris's specialist *maisons closes* for gay men. At the famous *l'Hôtel Marigny*, he made a deal with the brothel managers to allow him to spy on the crème de la crème of society through a small window as they enjoyed steam baths or erotic torture sessions; scenes that would later appear in his writing.

How to Spot a Former *Maison Close*

If you were a 'gentleman' of the Belle Époque on the lookout for a *maison close*, you would have kept an eye on the number plates above Paris's doors. If they were slightly larger, more colourful, and if the doorframe was noticeably elaborate, you would know it was a house of pleasure. And they weren't just limited to the red-light district.

If you happen to walk past No. 36 *rue Saint-Sulpice* in the posh 6th arrondissement, you'll notice the unusual style of the building and its doorway are vastly different from the others. Sitting just across from the famous Saint-Sulpice church, this was Miss Betty's brothel, a famous bordello that specialised in dominatrix role play. Priests in particular were allegedly drawn to the 'crucifixion parlour' and the 'Satan's Hell' torture room.

Rue Blanche

Three former brothels where you can now hang out

1 Maison Souquet, pg. 97
2 Hôtel Amour, pg. 113
3 Le Pigalle, pg. 114

Swingers' Club

Les Chandelles, hidden in the 1st arrondissement, is one of Paris's most exclusive swingers' clubs. Best suited for adventurous couples looking for an erotic and sensual evening inside the likes of a courtesan's boudoir. Let the unmistble minty smell in the air guide you there.

(*1 rue Thérèse, 1er, les-chandelles.com/language/en/; open every evening until 5am*)

Burlesque on a Boat

Find the Parisian equivalent to Dita Von Teese aboard a péniche parked across from Notre Dame Cathedral. Below the deck of *La Nouvelle Seine* there's a red velvet theatre where a talented and most glamorous troupe of burlesque artists put on an enchanting and memorable show at the weekends from 11pm.

(*3 Quai de Montebello, 5ème; check the Cabaret Burlesque calendar on cabaret-burlesque.com/category/calendrier*)

The Last Queen of Pigalle

Chez Michou is the campest cabaret in town, and has been since 1968. Hosted by Michou, an eighty-something former Parisian pop star best known for his covers of Brigitte Bardot and France Gall hits, here you can meet the queens that once ruled Pigalle. After serving you a surprisingly good dinner, the waiters become the entertainers and female impersonators, and the tiny restaurant their stage. Insanely kitsch and great fun.

(*80 rue des Martyrs, 18ème; +33 1 46 06 16 04; michou.com; open every day for dinner at 8.15pm, show starts at 10.30pm*)

Rocky Horror Picture Show à la Parisienne

Since the early 1970s, **Studio Galande** has been known for its indie and cult film screenings, but one American import in particular found a loyal Parisian fanbase at this tiny picture house in the Latin Quarter. For nearly forty years, *The Rocky Horror Picture Show* has been projected here twice a week in its original language, alongside the theatre's resident troupe of performers who shadow the film onstage, as is the tradition for the iconic 'midnight movie'. Somewhere between a striptease and musical theatre, it's still a sell-out show every Friday and Saturday after all these years, so book tickets in advance and don't forget to bring a bag of rice!

(*42 Rue Galande, 5ème; +33 1 43 26 94 08; tickets €12; show starts at 10pm; reserve online via studiogalande.fr*)

Cour de Rohan

09

My Last Ten Hours in Paris

Hey Nessy,

I'm stopping over in your town next week for a whopping ten hours on a quick layover. If I look for advice in the usual guides, they'll no doubt have me queuing up at some predictable landmark, eating steak frites at an overpriced tourist trap and heading back to the airport feeling pretty unfulfilled. I'd like to know, if it was the last ten hours you had left to spend in your city before it was lost to you forever, what would you do with that time? Not to be a downer.
    Thanks in advance.

Yours,
Pat

While the thought of only having ten hours left in Paris sends my soul whimpering into a corner with its tail between its legs, I'll rise to your challenge. I think if my time came to an end in this city, I'd want to go back to the very beginning and revisit the Paris I fell in love with. So I'd like to propose a walk through the quintessential backstreets of the Left Bank. We'll dip over to the other side of the river too, but dispel yourself of any notions that you're going to see everything. That's what the rest of this book is for, when you have a little more time. This is a taste of the Paris that captured my imagination, the Paris that makes me daydream and the Paris that I just couldn't live without...

Your Starting Point

We start at a time-capsule bistro on the Seine. Serving presidents and painters since 1851, the **Café Louis Philippe** is precisely the memory you'll want to have of eating at a Parisian café. But don't send yourself into a food coma; we have a lot of walking ahead of us. Order some charcuterie, a glass of wine and sit under the striped awnings surrounded by flower-laden window boxes and wrought-iron lanterns, until you're ready to tear yourself away and embark on our afternoon walk.

(*66 Quai de l'Hôtel de ville, 4ème; +33 1 42 72 29 42; cafelouisphilippe.com*)

Island Life

Cross the Pont Louis Phillippe over to the **Île Saint-Louis**, one of the two natural islands of the river Seine that is connected to the rest of Paris by four bridges. As you first set foot on the island, which was once used for grazing market cattle and storing wood, take the staircase down to the riverbanks on your right at the end of the bridge.

I had my first kiss in Paris at the end of the Quai de Bourbon, on the tip of the island, sitting on the bench under the glow of the lamp post. Stay a while to see the boats pass at the fork in the river; it's a special place to watch the world go by.

Café Louis Philippe

Explore the rest of the island if you like before taking another bridge over to the second island, **Île de la Cité** via the Pont Saint-Louis, where a street pianist or saxophonist will serenade you as you cross.

Wave to Notre Dame and take a stroll through her back garden, but we don't have time to queue up for a look inside, so make your way over the **Pont de l'Archevêche** to land on Paris proper again. At the end of the bridge, swing around to look back and take in the gorgeous view of the cathedral and the vines creeping over the wall down to the water.

Tip: If you need to unload some hand luggage during your stopover, there's a convenient 24-hour **City Locker** just ahead at 6 *rue des Bernadins*.

Quartier Latin Backstreets

Discover the artistry of an antique book that catches your eye among the green boxes of *les Bouquinistes* on **Quai de la Tournelle**, the riverside booksellers who have been trading along the Seine since the sixteenth century. Crossing the road into the *rue Maître-Albert*, take a quick right before the building with the painted ghost signs (look up) and follow the *rue Grand Degrés* until you reach a picture-perfect enclave where you can often find me under the string lights, drinking rosé on a warm summer's eve at the **Café Beaurepaire**. If you're tempted to stay for a glass on this charming little triangle of Parisian pavement, I won't blame you. (*1 rue de la Bûcherie, 5ème; +33 1 43 29 73 57; open Tues- Sun, 12pm-10.30pm*)

Île Saint-Louis

Rue Saint Julien le Pauvre

Moving on down the *rue de la* Bûcherie, cross over at the end of the road into the gardens of **Square René Viviani**, where the oldest tree in Paris resides, precariously leaning over in its old age. It is believed to have been planted in 1601. Exit on the other side at *rue Saint-Julien le Pauvre*, a picturesque cobblestone street with a medieval-style olive green building at one end and the famous Shakespeare & Co. bookshop waiting around the corner at the other (pg. 32). As I mentioned in the first chapter of this book, I prefer to visit the iconic store at night, when it's calm and tourists don't know it's open, but if you're in need of a quick souvenir, make a dash for it and meet me back here in ten.

Turn right at the olive green house next to Odette bakery on to *rue Galande*, one of the oldest streets in Paris, which becomes *rue St Severin* after you cross over a busy intersection. You can peer into the peaceful gardens of a medieval monastery around the back of the church on *rue des Prêtres Saint-Séverin*. Wander a little further down the road, and in the corner of your eye on the right, you'll spy the **Abbey Bookshop**, the off-the-beaten path alternative to Shakespeare & Co.

Take this little alleyway and then a right onto *rue de la Harpe*, where restaurants with red-chequered tablecloths try to lure you in for an overprice fondue. Don't be fooled – we're briefly passing through a touristy patch of the old Latin Quarter. Veer left, still on *rue de la Harpe*, until you exit the narrow backstreets, out into the open on the *Place Saint-Michel*. Throw a penny into the fountain or into the hat of a street performer, but let's not dwell amongst the crowds. Disappear through the arches on the opposite side of the *Place Saint-Michel* behind the green newspaper kiosk, next to the red awnings of Le Rive Gauche café.

We're entering the unexpected calm of *rue de l'Hirondelle*, an ancient route of the Left Bank of Paris which used to be much longer until General Haussmann amputated nearly half of it to make way for the grandiose *Place Saint-Michel* we just left behind. No. 25 is home to a legendary absinthe bar with a drinking cave that dates back to the year 1290, called **La Vénus Noire** (pg. 18).

Secrets of Saint-Germain

Take a left and then a right onto *rue Saint-André des Arts*, where you might be tempted by the aromas escaping the Créperie Saint-Germain at No. 33. A few metres up the road, stop in front of a beautiful green door at No. 52. I remember when my mother once sent me a text message that simply read: '52 *rue Saint-André des Arts*. Fab courtyard, door open.' In Paris, 'door open' essentially means that the door to the building doesn't require an entry code during the week – you just have to press the main button on the keypad and you're in. This usually applies to most buildings that have public offices inside them like this one – an unexpected hidden stunner well worth poking your head into.

We're en route to an even more secret courtyard – so secret we might not even be able to get inside, but believe me, it's worth a try. I used to go there often with a little picnic for myself when I first arrived in Paris, totally besotted with this city I now called home. Then one day, I returned only to find the gates to my little paradise had been closed to visitors – indefinitely. Apparently local residents had made a few complaints about people just hanging around and eating lunch there. *Oops.* Well, you asked me what I would do if I had ten final hours in Paris – you'd better believe I would find my way back into that courtyard, one last time. Just remember, we have to be discreet, respectful and this will work much better if we're no more than two. Trying it alone is ideal. At No. 61 *rue Saint-André des Arts*, just before The Mazet, the pub where Jim Morrison was last spotted publicly the day before he died, duck into the archway down the uneven cobblestones of **Cour du Commerce Saint-André**.

On your right, in between the buildings at No. 2 and No. 4, you'll find the gate to **Cour de Rohan**. Now it's time to wait. Have a little patience and a smile at the ready, and wait for one of the residents or a delivery person to emerge and kindly let us in after them, '*juste pour un moment*'.

I've never had to hang around more than fifteen minutes for someone to let me in, but while you wait, you could always plant yourself on the terrace of **Café Procope**, the oldest café in continuous operation in Paris. If you're with someone who can guard your belongings (and your glass of wine), there are a few tables directly facing the gate which make for the perfect stakeout, close enough to make a run for it.

(*3 Cour du Commerce Saint-André, 6ème; procope.com; open every day, 11.45am–midnight*)

Left: Rue de l'Hirondelle
Below: Rue Saint-André
des Arts

When you do make it inside this cherished place, time stops and everything outside ceases to exist. Wild ivy, pink stone, ancient wooden doors, mysterious staircases to fairy-tale residences; it will make you dizzy with adoration.

The series of courtyards, each more beautiful than the previous, date back as far as the fourteenth century and even contain a piece of the oldest wall of Paris, which King Louis Phillippe had built to protect the city circa 1200. The beauty of a forgotten world, so delicately preserved in this gated oasis hidden away in the centre of Paris, is enough to bring you to tears. When you're ready to leave, just look for the button at the side to buzz you out.

Leaving the cobblestone street the same way you came in, the *rue Saint-André des Arts* ends at the bustling market scene of *rue de Buci*. Stop for some roses or an English newspaper at the old yellow storefront of Buci News before heading back in the direction of the Seine up *rue Dauphine*. At No. 30, we'll take a shortcut through the buildings via the *Passage Dauphine*, where you'll find a charming teahouse serving cakes, appropriately named **L'Heure Gourmande** (pg. 124). You'll emerge from the passage to take a right along *rue Mazarine*, known for its historic fine art galleries. Painter Édouard Manet lived at No. 60.

Have an Oliver Twist moment, breathing heavily against the window display of Michelin-star chef Guy Savoy's Left Bank bakery, **Goût de Brioche**. Specialising in sweet and savoury buns or large brioche for 6-8 people (or just you), the smell of caramelised butter and parmesan is too good to resist.
(*54 rue Mazarine, 6ème; goutdebrioche.com; open Wed-Sun, 8.30am-7.30pm*)

Right: Cour de Rohan

Opposite: Goût de Brioche

The top of the road bends around the secluded **Square Gabriel Perné**, a public garden with stone benches sculpted like open books and pink cherry blossom trees in bloom during the spring. Where the road comes to end, poke your head into the little blue bookstore **Librairie des Alpes**, filled with, you guessed it, anything alpine-related. They have some beautiful vintage posters promoting tourism in the French Alps for sale too.

(*6 rue de Seine, 6ème; librairie-des-alpes.com; open Tues-Sat, 12pm-7pm*)

Smart Souvenirs

We're just steps away from the river Seine again now, where you'll find more green boxes filled with vintage books and art prints to browse. This might actually be my favourite cluster of *les bouquinistes*, here on the **Quai Malaquais**.

Stop for a breather at the charming little **Café des Beaux Arts** on the corner (*7 Quai Malaquais, 6ème; cafe-des-beaux-arts.com; open every day, 7am-2am*) or continue on down the ***rue Bonaparte*** back into the heart of Saint-Germain des Près.

I never walk down this street without entering the world of **Officine Universelle Buly 1803**. Modelled after a traditional nineteenth-century French pharmacy, with antique apothecary cabinets and gorgeous floor tiling, the decor of this jewel box of a shop is reason enough to enter. This Parisian perfume and cosmetics brand dates back 200 years, making it not the worst place in the city to pick up a scented candle or two for the gifts drawer. In fact, these candles are just about the most luxurious little souvenirs of Paris you could come away with.

Pore over the beautiful vintage packaging and don't miss the drawers full of natural honeycomb sponges, boar-bristle brushes and traditional boxwood combs. Go on, spoil yourself or someone else.

(*6 rue Bonaparte, 6ème; buly1803.com; open Mon-Sat, 10am-7pm*)

Make a right onto *rue Jacob*, looking out for the **Hôtel d'Angleterre** at No. 44, where Ernest Hemingway and his first wife Hadley stayed in room 14 for their first night in Paris, in December 1921. It was then called the Hôtel Jacob, and before that, the building was the location of the British Embassy, hence the name of the hotel today. The pioneering aviator Charles Lindbergh also stayed here after completing the world's first non-stop solo flight from New York to Paris in 1927. There's a beautiful little courtyard behind the façade worth a peek. Take a card at reception for your next visit and ask for a look around.

One building over at No. 48, push open the door to the mad and wonderful world of **Librairie Alain Brieux**. Specialising in medical and rare anatomy ephemera, scientific instruments, strange objects and antique botanical prints since 1958, be prepared to wonder where the time went.
(*48 rue Jacob, 6ème; alainbrieux.com; open Mon-Fri, 10am-6.30pm, Sat, 2pm-6.30pm, daily lunchtime closing, 1pm-2pm*)

Nearly there... (there's wine and cheese at the finish line)
Let's pick up the pace and turn left onto *rue du Pré aux Clercs*, admiring the colourful window boxes decorating the façade of **Le Saint Hôtel** as you walk by. Veer to the right on the *rue Saint-Guillaume*, which will lead you out onto my favourite stretch of the famed *boulevard Saint-Germain*. Pay special attention to the pretty façade and enviable terrace of No. 218 above a charming umbrella boutique. When you reach a crossing with *rue Saint-Thomas d'Aquin*, look to your right to see the stunning seventeenth-century Catholic church just casually hidden behind the boulevard. Stroll down to the little roundabout and back up to feel like you've popped over to a miniature piazza in Rome for a minute. On the other side of the boulevard, there's another little treasure worth discovering down the *rue de Luynes*. About halfway down, there's a gorgeous art nouveau cul-de-sac called **Square de Luynes**. I could live on the concierge's

stoop at No. 3. Where *boulevard Saint-Germain* comes to an end, cross diagonally over the intersection to the left and head down the *rue Paul-Louis Courier*, poking your head down the little alleyway at No. 11 and then turning left again onto the charming **rue de Saint-Simon**. Do a sweep of the whole street (it's not very long), first checking out the neo-gothic mansion at No. 2, that exotic atelier behind the gate at No. 11 and the quaint little courtyard in front of the Hôtel Duc de Saint-Simon at No. 14.

We come to the last part of our walk, turning right on **rue de Grenelle**, admiring the rows of stunning mansions and Hôtel Particuliers one after another, today mostly serving as official government buildings and embassies. If you still have time to spare, follow the signs at the end of the road to the **Musée Rodin** on your left. It's a classic, perfect museum housed in a palatial mansion overlooking one of the finest gardens in Paris.
(*79 rue de Varenne, 7ème; musee-rodin.fr; open Tues- Sun, 10am-5.45pm, and until 8.45pm on Wed*)

You might have noticed the Eiffel Tower poking its head out over the trees. I'm not suggesting we climb up the tower, but something much better. First we'll need some wine and cheese (I think you can guess where this is heading). Okay, quick detour. We need to hunt down a special cheese shop, which is a brisk five-minute walk to the right of the big gold dome where Napoleon's tomb is housed. Cross the *Place des Invalides* and take the *avenue de la Motte-Picquet*, where you'll find the most incredible display of the smelly stuff at **Fromagerie Griffon**.
(*23 bis avenue de la Motte-Picquet, 7ème; +331 45 50 14 85; Tues-Sat, 9.30am-7.30pm*)

Cheese in the bag, now let's head back up towards the river and grab a bottle of vino. Stick to the left side of the lawns of Invalides on **rue Fabert** and take a left

Port des Champs-Élysées
on the banks of the Seine

onto *rue Saint-Dominique*, where you'll find a *Nicolas* wine shop on the corner.
Ask them to uncork the bottle for you before you leave.
(*25 boulevard de la Tour-Maubourg, 7ème; nicolas.com; open Mon-Sat*)

Take a right outside the shop up the **boulevard de la Tour Maubourg** which
brings you to the Seine. The end of this walk is finally in sight. Take the Pont des
Invalides just in front of you over to the other side and pick a spot along the
riverbanks of **Porte des Champs-Élysées** to share your cheese and wine picnic
with the Eiffel Tower. I suggest dangling your legs above the water between the
Pont des Invalides and the Pont Alexandre III, next to a little houseboat called
the *Louise*. And if you didn't enjoy all of our Parisian stroll, at least you can say
you drank wine and ate *fromage* in front of the *Tour Eiffel*.

While Paris is Sleeping
Flight's been delayed? If you find yourself in Paris at odd hours, wondering where
you can still get an authentic bite to eat, head to **Chez Denise**, the place to go for
late night French fare. It's the place where chefs congregate after dinner service,
looking for a major steak tartare. Wine is charged according to how much you
drink and comes in nondescript glass carafes, and until seven in the morning,
you can try their slow-cooked beef stew with French fries for dipping (great for
soaking up one too many cocktails). The chocolate Labrador behind the bar is
the mascot of the joint, but don't expect overly friendly or chatty waiters – this
place embodies everything romantically gritty about French waiters.
(*5 Rue des Prouvaires, 1er; open Mon-Fri for lunch & dinner until 5am*)

Grand Mosque of Paris

10

Forget 'Pinterest' Paris

Dear Nessy,

This is not going to be your typical email asking for travel tips. In the past few years, I feel like we've witnessed the media's portrayal of Paris change from a chocolate-box city of adorable delights to a veritable 'no-go zone'. I fear I'm almost falling victim to the fear-mongering and the hysteria about Europe myself. So to snap myself out of it, I've chosen your city as my next destination, but I want to seek out the other side of Paris, discover the diversity and generally skip the French clichés that can be so unproductive when travelling. The problem is, I honestly have no idea where to start and I was quite surprised at how little information the usual Paris guidebooks provide on this type of experience. I've always been a visitor, not a tourist. When I go somewhere, I'd rather spend the trip soaking up the soul of a place instead of climbing on some tour bus to see a city fly by without any meaningful contact. Can you point me in the right direction?

Anxiously awaiting your reply,
Sage

Whenever one of those French perfume commercials come on the television, I have to roll my eyes. Hotel balconies with Eiffel Tower views, baby blue macarons and beret-wearing 'locals' – no, this is not the real Paris. Sure, that stuff makes for a pretty Pinterest board, but this city has a whole different layer of beauty in its diversity. Paris can be the aroma of saffron that wraps around you as you cycle down the boulevard or the sound of excited schoolchildren clutching their after-school snacks outside the kosher bakery owned by a Tunisian family. It can be Sunday afternoon tea and cakes at the mosque, date night at the local West African grill, and entire neighbourhoods where French is the second language.

Following the tragic attacks on Paris in November 2015, Fox News described these parts of Paris as 'no-go zones'. My response to that is simply this: if you were to follow their advice, you would be missing out on some of the most vibrant and interesting neighbourhoods this city has to offer. Their misjudgement would deprive you of a delectable voyage through the last remnants of genuine working-class village life in Paris. These are places where you don't need a passport to discover a feast of culture from all around the world, and I couldn't be more excited to be accompanying you on this journey.

Out of Africa

The neighbourhood of **la Goutte d'Or** ('drop of gold') gets its name from the wine which was produced there until the nineteenth century, when central Paris didn't yet include what was then still just fields and vineyards. It was a prize-winning wine gifted to the king on his birthday by the city of Paris. Hidden in the backstreets of la Goutte d'Or, you can still find traces of this forgotten little wine country, but we'll get to that a bit later.

The settlement of la Goutte d'Or came in many waves. The first communities to make a home for themselves here were the provincial workers, who came to find jobs in the capital's factories spawned by the Industrial Revolution. Then came a wave of European migrants – Belgian, Italian, Polish and Spanish – followed by the exiles of colonisation in the 1950s, a North African community that still holds a strong presence in the area. Finally in the '80s, Sub-Saharan Africans found their way to la Goutte d'Or to add their own flavours to this multicultural melting pot. Thanks to these two communities sharing this little patch of Paris, today it doesn't take more than a few minutes to stroll between North and West Africa by foot.

Métro to the Maghreb

Stepping off the métro at Barbès-Rochechouart is like disembarking from an airplane that lands you right in the middle of a bustling street market in the Maghreb. Every Wednesday and Saturday, the **Marché Barbès** sets up along the *boulevard de la Chapelle*, directly under the elevated train tracks as the métro rumbles overhead. Get ready to enter a world of colourful chaos, where, if gravity is not your strong suit, you might just get swept up with the human tide of bargain hunters, burrowing through boxes of cut-price housewares and stockpiling on olives and avocados by the kilo. Everything here is sold at half the price you'll find in any other market in the city. Put away your fancy camera (this is not that kind of market) and just soak in the insatiable energy of this unapologetic and ungentrified parade of Parisian diversity.

Wine Country

Such a lively introduction to the *quartier* perhaps requires a moment to catch your breath before we continue our journey to West Africa, so let's find a hidden oasis harking back to the peaceful vineyards that once dominated this corner of Paris. Head a few minutes north up the *boulevard Barbès* from the station and take the first right turn onto *rue de la Goutte d'Or* – I promise, there's a real treat in store behind an iron gate at **No. 42: Villa Poissonnière**. (The gates are usually open, especially at lunchtime, but if they happen to be closed, just wait around for a resident to come in or out.)

An unexpected country road lost in time, away from the market vendors' calls, the only noise here is that of chirping birds and the rustling of leaves. Each nineteenth-century house lining the cobblestone alleyway has its own pocket-sized front garden filled with potted plants and overgrown vines. When the Goutte d'Or was still just open countryside, vineyards and wineries, this site dating back to 1840 is said to have been the property of a wine grower. Close your eyes and try to picture it: the farmer watching over his grapes from his villa amongst the vines.

Head back out onto the *rue Goutte d'Or* and continue up the street until the next left turn on *rue des Gardes*, where you can take a tour of **Square Léon**, a small park and a peaceful neighbourhood hang-out. You'll find the locals playing checkers and kids playing basketball (entrance to the court at 25 *rue des Gardes*). Behind the square is the Église de Saint-Bernard de la Chapelle, where in 1996, more than 300 protesters and humanitarians occupied the church and staged a hunger strike to protect African workers without work permits. It was a big media story that summer, winning the hearts of Parisians, but after two months of protest, ultimately the police stormed the church and rounded up the workers.

African Haute Couture

At the opposite end of the Square Léon, take the *rue Léon*, the gateway to the heart of West Africa in Paris, three blocks north to the ***rue Doudeauville***. You might have already noticed the colourful West African wax fabric stores in the area, and this street has some of the best. Witness African couture in the making behind the hand-painted storefront of **No. 29 La Beauté des Femmes**, one of many boutiques you'll find in the area specialising in Batik wax textiles. Each fabric and pattern has its own meaning to communicate information about the women that traditionally wear them. For example, a print with chickens, chicks, and rooster heads, hints that the wearer may have a husband, but that she's the true head of the family (and in some regions that he's physically useless). A woman who takes special pride in her education might wear a print featuring letters, chalkboards, measuring sticks and books.

These fabrics are a testament to African ingenuity, creativity and cultural pride, and have played a big role in the lives of African women over generations. Recently, Batik fabrics have featured in collections by European fashion designers such as Jean Paul Gaultier and Dries van Noten.

(*Further reading on MessyNessyChic.com, 'The Chanel of Africa'*.)

The Tailor of *rue de Panama*

Take a left onto *rue des Poissonniers* and turn into *rue de Panama*, where you'll find **La Sape & Co.**, the unofficial Parisian headquarters of *les Sapeurs* (literally: the dressers), a subculture of extraordinarily dressed dandies from the Congo. The story of les Sapeurs is one quite special to me, one that first sparked my curiosity for the off-beat and unique subcultures of this earth, and one that I will probably follow for the rest of my life.

When you think of silk handkerchiefs, pink corduroys, tweed and double-breasted tailoring, do you associate such a style of dress with some of the poorest slums of Africa? Despite having witnessed first-hand the brutality and horror of three civil wars, a Congolese *Sapeur* doesn't settle for anything less than a tailored suit as he strolls the impoverished streets in immaculate Italian footwear, elegantly smoking his mahogany pipe.

Sapologie is not a fashion trend. It serves as something closer to a religion; a code of living. They are known as a non-violent people, respectful and considerate towards others. One of their mottos is, 'Let's drop the weapons, let us work and dress elegantly.' Of course, they must also have the sartorial know-how. Socks should be a certain height, a maximum of three colours can be used in one outfit, and an attention to detail is required, such as leaving the bottom cuff button of a suit jacket undone. The tell-tale difference between an off-the-rack suit and a tailored one is buttonholes that you can actually undo. These are all valuable tips you can learn from *les Sapeurs* and they consider their style as an art form – the art of being a gentleman.

Most *Sapeurs* dream of making it to Paris, which they see as the 'promised land' of haute 'sapeurism'. One sapeur who did make it over is Jocelyn Armel, who owns this fashion boutique, La Sape & Co., selling dandy suits, tweeds and accessories in every colour under the rainbow. A well-respected figure in Paris's West African community, he acts as a sort of ambassador for this style subculture in Europe, also referred to as *La Sape*, which is short for *Société des Ambianceurs et des Personnes Élégantes* ('Society of Tastemakers and Elegant People'). Mr Armel, known amongst his dandy peers as '*Le Bachelor*', says their goal is 'to celebrate good fashion sense and an ideal of "gentlemanly" behaviour. We as Africans need to believe in Africa again, we need to believe that something good can come out of the continent and its people.'

When I ask if I can take his picture, he jumps at the chance to do an elaborate costume change just for me. Don't be shy, pay this passionate tailor of *rue de Panama* a visit, and observe the lively scene that often congregates outside his boutique, opposite a hairdresser dedicated to Barack Obama.
(*12 rue de Panama, 18ème; usually open Tues-Sun afternoons until 8pm*)

Heart of West Africa

Come back out onto the *rue des Poissonniers*, cross over to the Haitian wig shop and keep walking left until you get to a corner store with the vintage ghost sign for charcuterie. Turn right here into the **Marché Dejean**, where a procession of market vendors gather on this little pedestrian street to take over your senses with their perfumed and colourful stalls. In la Goutte d'Or, locals can shop for fresh tilapia fish and barracuda from Africa, tropical vegetables like manioc or okra, and various essential products for a traditional African feast.
(*rue Dejean, 18ème; Tues-Sun*)

Senegalese Soul Food

You must be famished by now, so it's time to seek out a humble neighbourhood favourite for homemade Senegalese cuisine. Head back over to the other side of *boulevard Barbès* to the parallel street, *rue de Clignancourt*, where **Les Délices du Sacré-Cœur** serves up enormous and delicious traditional dishes for just €5 each. If you haven't tried African food before, the staff are really kind and helpful. I recommend the *maffe*, a beautiful stew made with tender chicken, fish or lamb, simmered in a fragrant sauce, thickened with ground peanuts and served alongside plantain, chunky carrots and rice. For something 'lighter', go for the chicken or fish *yassa*, beautifully marinated in lemon and onions. Don't forget to try the homemade ginger or hibiscus drinks for an extra euro.
(*52 bis, rue de Clignancourt; +33 6 46 55 58 14; open Mon-Sun for lunch & dinner*)

The Shoe Theatre

On your way back towards the métro, you must stop in at the most surreal shoe shop in Paris. Hiding behind the banal façade of **Kata**, a bargain shoe bazaar where you can shop endless piles of moccasins, pumps and boots for as little as €3 a pair, you'll find an extraordinary forgotten old theatre. Shoppers roam the aisles where the audience once sat in the stalls, surrounded by ionic columns, neo-classical balconies, gilded mouldings and red velvet curtains – there are even still advertising posters from the Belle Époque on the staircase, harshly lit under the modern neon lighting. Built in 1914 as one of the movie palaces of yesteryear, le Barbès Palace could accommodate up to 1,200 spectators but it sadly ended its film career as an adult cinema in the '80s before permanently bringing down the curtain and finding a second life in limbo as this discount shoe store.

(*34 boulevard Barbès, 18ème; Mon-Sat, 11am-7.30pm*)

There's a happier ending down the road, next to the métro, for **Le Louxor** cinema, a 1920s Egyptian revival-style movie palace that was abandoned, and stood lifeless and ignored for more than twenty years at the busy cross-section of *boulevard Barbès*. Just as the bulldozer was setting its sights on the old movie palace, a neighbourhood association came to its rescue and campaigned for the city to restore the historical building to its former glory. In 2013, this legend of pre-war entertainment was awoken from its slumber and its screens lit up once

Left: Le Louxor
Below: Kata

again. With a brand new facelift, the theatre has become a hub of independent foreign-language films from Asia, Latin America and Africa. If you buy a ticket, there's a beautiful gilded art deco bar and terrace with a view to finish your excursion in Paris's Goutte D'Or.
(*170 boulevard Magenta, 18ème; open every day, film times on cinemalouxor.fr*)

Around the World in a Few Arrondissements

Dining in the Souk

Try to resist plunging your hands into the colourful barrels of spices that greet you upon your arrival at **Le Souk**. You could be in Marrakech, entering a spice shop in the marketplace. The couscous is as fluffy as it should be and you won't regret trying the pigeon pastilla (a sweet and salty pie) and aubergine caviar at this atmospheric Moroccan gem.

(*1 rue Keller, 11ème; +33 1 49 29 05 08; Tues-Sun for lunch & dinner*)

Tea at Twilight in a Hero's Mosque

Did you ever hear about that time the **Grand Mosque of Paris** helped Jews escape the Nazis by giving them Muslim IDs? Perhaps not. An untold 'Oscar Schindler' story buried beneath the fortress of mosaics and tranquil gardens occupying an entire city block in the Latin Quarter, the mosque's underground caverns once served as a refuge for resistance fighters and French Jews, where they could be provided with certificates of Muslim identity. Meanwhile upstairs, the wise Algerian-born religious leader Kaddour Benghabrit, the 'Schindler' in our story, was giving tours of the mosque to Nazi officers and their wives, unaware of who was hiding under their feet.

A North African and Jewish resistance fighter named Albert Assouline, who had escaped from a German prison camp, wrote about his experience hiding in the mosque: 'No fewer than 1,732 resistance fighters found refuge in its

Right: Grand Mosque of
Paris courtyard
Opposite: Le Souk

underground caverns. These included Muslim escapees but also Christians and Jews. The latter were by far the most numerous.' Giving sanctuary to Jews was largely impulsive and was never an organised movement by the mosque, which is perhaps why historical records remain so bleary, but I recommend a recent French film, *Les Hommes Libres* (*Free Men*), that brings to light this remarkable true story.

Today, the mosque in the 5th arrondissement also plays host to one of the most charming cafés in Paris, housed within two leafy courtyards, both covered in mosaics (the first at the front of house and the second on the other side, past the bakery stand). The energetic waiters are always ready to ceremoniously pour you more fresh mint tea to accompany those syrupy Arabic pastries. It's very popular with Parisian families on Sunday afternoons, but it's not a place tourists are very aware of. The café is also open until midnight for tea under the stars while contemplating the fascinating history within its walls.
(*1 rue Daubenton, 5ème; +33 1 15 35 97 33; open every day, 9am to midnight, last service at 10.30pm*)

Silk Road Salon

Hidden in plain sight amongst the trendy hipster cafés along the Canal Saint-Martin, push open the door of the **Centre Culturel Pouya** and enter a peaceful Iranian tea salon, a place to read a book, enjoy a poetry reading or catch up on some work amongst beautiful Persian carpets, cushions, books and perfumes of the Silk Road. Highlighting Persian art and culture, the Pouya centre brings together students of all ages, looking to learn, taste and feel something truly unique in Paris.
(*48 Quai de Jemmapes, 10ème; pouya.org; Mon-Sat, 11am-11pm, and Sunday, 2pm-9pm*)

Centre Culturel Pouya

A Good Scrub for the Weary Traveller

There's something about your first trip to the hammam that makes you feel like you've undergone a rite of passage. Mind you, it also leaves you with skin that feels like that of a new-born baby, and it's a far more interesting and entertaining experience than at your typical western spa. Paris has a lot of hammams, and before I recommend any, let me just pass on a few first-timer tips for navigating them. There are usually five stages to a hammam experience: cleansing, bathing, steaming, massage and lastly, rest. Once you've signed in and got yourself to the steam room, attendants will fetch you when it's time for your various treatments, which usually includes getting lathered in black soap and an exfoliation scrub on a marble table, as well as a massage if you've opted for it. Try not to worry about knowing what to do or where to be or how to act – all you should really be doing is lying around. However, if you're the type that gets shy undressing in your gym's locker room, this is probably not an activity for you, nor would it be if you're terribly sensitive to heat or exfoliation. The entire process of steaming, cooling, cleansing and getting scrubbed to within an inch of your life (known as *le gommage*) usually takes about forty-five minutes. Most hammams provide paper underwear that cover the critical parts, but bring your own swimsuit and flip-flops just in case. There might be a jacuzzi.

The 1920s **Hammam de la Mosquée de Paris** is the most beautiful, authentic and affordable choice, at around €30 for entry plus *gommage*, but it's also one of the busiest, which makes it less of a place to relax in a sleepy daze afterwards. If you're limited on time, it's perfect.
(*39 rue Geoffroy-Saint-Hilaire, 5ème; restaurantauxportesdelorient.com; 10am-9pm; reserved for women Wed-Sat, and for men Tues- Sun*)

The **O'Kari** hammam is the sort of place you reserve for a special occasion such as a birthday or a hen do; it's exclusively for women and hidden in a charming courtyard. An altogether more gentle and luxurious experience, from €59.
(*22 rue Dussoubs, 2ème; +33 1 41 36 94 66; O-kari.com; Mon-Sat*)

Little India

One of the longest covered streets in Paris near Gare de l'Est, ***Passage Brady*** is a little piece of India where the air smells of exotic spices, fruits, oils and teas. You can find small food markets selling speciality produce, hundreds of fragrant spices and rices, and it's also fun to shop for authentic brightly coloured fashion, kitschy decor, jewellery and other Indian goods sourced from far away. The choice of inexpensive South Asian restaurants here can be a little overwhelming, especially with the cheery waiters promising you the best chicken vindaloo in Paris at every turn. A simple, 'perhaps later' ('*peut-etre plus tard*') is usually enough to keep the catchers happy, but the one to save your

Passage Brady

appetite for is **Pooja**. A truly good Indian meal is hard to come by in this city (compared to London, for example), but Parisians flock to Pooja for its fresh, authentic cuisine, friendly welcome and the al fresco Indian summer ambience, thanks to the 'outdoor' seating under the glass roof of *Passage Brady*. Perfect for first-timers and vegetarians too, and even the most experienced curry enthusiasts will be pleasantly surprised.

(*91 Passage Brady, 11ème; +33 1 48 24 00 83; Mon-Sat for lunch & dinner, Sun dinner only*)

Belleville: A Beautiful Rebel Town

There will always be an air of rebellion up in Belleville, the wine-making village built on a hill that turned into a hotbed of working-class radicalism during the Paris Commune of 1871, when almost half the neighbourhood was wiped out in a bloody rebellion against the French government. Belleville is still home to the headquarters of the French Communist Party, and until only very recently, if you were to spend time in the neighbourhood, you would have detected a different Parisian accent, even a deviating dialect, spoken only by the locals. Karl Marx himself was inspired by the revolutionary Parisian workers who fought against a 'dictatorship of the proletariat', and it's been said that the Paris Commune acted like a blueprint for communism, at least, the sort of communism that would help defeat the Nazis, preached egalitarianism and women's rights. At the top of the hill, in between historic artists' ateliers, we can still find the tell-tale signs of this rebellious country village, where traditional folk songs were the soundtrack to the people's struggle, and where, according to legend, the quartier's most famous resident, Edith Piaf, was born under a streetlight on the corner of *rue de Belleville*.

Commune Graffiti

To know before you go

To take a real, unfiltered glimpse into modern-day Belleville, we must start at the bottom.

Today, at the foot of the hill, you'll find one of Paris's Chinatowns, sharing a blurred border with a North African community, both of which wound up here with the arrival of twentieth-century migrants. They seem to coexist peacefully, despite some glaring ironies. On the main boulevard, where Chinese markets and Vietnamese restaurants alternate with Arabic pastry shops, Tunisian-Jewish coffee shops, and a growing presence of hipster cafés, there exists what you might call an elephant in the room. Come five or six o'clock in the evening, sometimes earlier, a tribe of overly glammed-up women, mostly of Asian origin, wearing miniskirts and patent leather boots à la *Pretty Woman*, take their places along the boulevard, fanning out from the Belleville métro stop. These hardened ladies of the night huddle together in groups of two or three, chatting away in Mandarin as if casually waiting for a bus, until they disappear one by one with a shadowy figure in tow into the backstreets of Belleville. They share this territory with the boulevard's ever-present gathering of North African elders having their own animated discussions in Arabic about local politics and news from back home. Paying no mind to each other, tolerating each other even, these two distant tribes make the unlikeliest of neighbours. I live a few stops down the métro line from Belleville on the opposite side of the Père Lachaise Cemetery and have come to know the quartier well, flaws and all. There's nothing fake or predictable about Belleville. It's my slightly unconventional neighbour that I couldn't live without.

Fuel up on Pho

Let's start by getting some grub to fuel us for an afternoon excursion up the hill. At least twice a week, you can find me at **Dong Huong**, a legendary Vietnamese canteen in Belleville; it has been run by the same extended family for twenty years, who happen to have a thing for dressing like American gangsters from the 1940s. The menu has pictures, the plates are plastic, but this place serves the best pho soup in Paris and for some reason it just feels like home. If you want to try something on the menu other than pho, I recommend going for the *Cha Tom* (B10 or B11); a do-it-yourself spring roll with all the ingredients laid out in front of you. (*14 rue Louis Bonnet, 11ème; dong-huong.fr; open every day except Tues, midday-10.30pm*)

The Street that gave birth to Edith Piaf

Bellies filled with broth and rice noodles, we begin our ascent up the *rue de Belleville*. The first landmark is the **Café Au Folies** at No. 8, an old cabaret music hall from a time when the area was still swarming with establishments serving tax-free wine. Edith Piaf sang here in her early days and today it's the quartier's cardinal dive bistrot, occupied by local bohemians who crowd onto the terrace, where no one will judge them for drinking too much wine (even well before 5 o'clock). The cobblestone alleyway to the left of the Folies, *rue Denoyez*, was until recently an infamous artists' squat, a rainbow of brightly coloured galleries and an open-air museum of street art covered in graffiti. In 2016, the town hall's patience for this Belleville misfit ran out. The last time I walked past, the bulldozers had already been sent in to make way for social housing and a children's nursery. Authorities have always tried to tame Belleville, but something tells me that as soon as the construction work is done, the graffiti and the artists will be back. Go have a look and see if I'm right.

Continuing up the *rue de Belleville*, notice the giant spiky durian fruit for sale outside Chinese grocery shops and the shop windows filled with imported porcelain, Buddha statues, firecrackers and colourful paper lanterns. One of my favourite stops is the **Bazar de Belleville**, where I can spend a good half hour stocking up on inexpensive kitschy accessories that I'll add to my bookshelf or hang in my bathroom. They also stock just about every practical household good you can think of for a quarter of the price – just don't expect it to last you a lifetime. (*51 rue de Belleville, 20ème*)

Before we veer off into the smaller streets, give a wave to Edith Piaf's childhood home at No. 72, where there's a commemorative plaque. If you have time later on, there's also an intimate museum further down the hill dedicated to the legendary French singer they called La Môme ('the kid') (pg. 73).

Belle View

Back-up a few doors and head down the *rue Piat*, looking out for a green gate on your right at No. 45, with the name **Villa Ottoz** written over the arch. Pass through the gates and take the leafy path; this was once a residential road lined with cottages and artists' villas on either side, until they fell victim to the wrecking ball of urbanisation in the 1960s and '70s. Veering to the left, you'll come to a staircase going down the hill. Just take a moment here at the top of the stairs to look into the distance. Do you see her there, to the right? It's one of my favourite unexpected views of the Eiffel Tower. This is the Parc de Belleville, created in the 1980s on the site of what was originally an old gypsum quarry. If you carry on along the path, you'll come to an opening in the trees and find the longest cascading fountain in Paris and panoramic views across the city. On the other side of the fountains, take the little path in between two staircases which leads you to a mini vineyard of Pinot Meunier and Chardonnay grapes. It should now start to make sense where Belleville got its name; it is derived from *belle vue*, literally 'beautiful view'.

Snooping like a Secret Agent

Back up on the *rue Piat*, follow the road as it slopes down to the right, stopping at **No. 16 Villa Castel**, an old nineteenth-century workers' residence. Spot the street-art tribute to Manet's 'Le Balcon' at the bottom right window of this ageing humpty dumpty brick façade. If you're patient and stealthy enough to sneak past the gate behind a resident on their way out, you'll find even more grape vines climbing up the wall. Just to the left of this yellow brick house is the peaceful **Passage Plantin**, one of the narrowest streets in Paris. Somehow, Hollywood found this little passage out of time and filmed a scene here for one of the *Jason Bourne* movies. If you're feeling secret-agent-like, I absolutely *don't* recommend using the drainpipes to get a better look over the fences, especially over the wall at No. 2. At the end of the alley, head down the staircase and look for the gate on your right hidden amongst the leaves. There's a beautiful, almost ancient staircase leading up to hidden house that's worth a peep.

Vive le Village

Emerge on the other end of *Passage Plantin* and take the *rue des Couronnes* back up the slope until you get to the roundabout **Place Henri Krasucki**, dedicated to a communist resistance fighter who fought during the German occupation of Paris. A resident of the building just off the roundabout at 107 *rue des Couronnes*, Krasucki survived deportation to both Auschwitz and then Buchenwald, and became the leader of the French Communist Party upon his return. We're in the true heart of Belleville's village now, but to get a real sense how it all looked fifty or even a hundred years ago, we should take the **rue des Cascades** to the left of the red café. Notice the beautiful gothic building at No. 70. If Romeo is still looking for Juliet, I think she's living in Belleville on the first floor of this unexpected backstreet gem. Continue on further down the road until you reach

Rue des Cascades

a row of colourful old-world shopfronts at the bend. The little stone house at the intersection is the oldest building in the entire arrondissement, built over a Gallo-Roman aqueduct for checking the system and cleanliness of the water. If the weather permits, take a seat on the makeshift terrace of **La Fontaine Henri IV**, in the nook of the sidewalk, and order a €3 glass of wine. Olives and cashew nuts will come eventually too; the service goes at a village's pace, but there's no rush at a magical place like this.

(*42 rue des Cascades, 20ème; open every afternoon until 2am*)

Maybe this spot should have been in my chapter about 'Paris, like it is in the Movies,' but it didn't seem right to take you here without giving you the backstory of Belleville. Cast your eyes over at the corner of the house directly opposite the café entrance. Do you see the carvings of those ghostly faces on the wall? Get a little closer and you'll see the words '*Vive la Commune*' carved around the skulls, referring to the radical socialist and revolutionary government that ruled Paris from 18 March to 28 May 1871. That was well over a century ago. These carvings are recent. So like I said, there will always be an air of rebellion up in Belleville.

Shortcuts!

It's raining, what can I do?
Take cover in the network of nineteenth-century covered passageways, perfect for rainy-day shopping. See 'Tunnels to the Belle Époque' (pg. 47).

I just need a good cup of coffee!
Get your fix at speciality coffee shops like Café Loustic (pg. 19), Boot Café (pg. 63), or Café Kitsuné (*51 Galerie de Montpensier, 1er, open every day, 10am–5pm*). And here's how to order the coffee you want wherever you are:

> A standard espresso without milk: *un café*
> Two shots of coffee to really wake you up: *un double espresso*
> A long filter coffee: *un café allongé*
> A machiatto (an espresso with a splash of hot milk): *une noisette*
> A bowl of steamed, frothy milk with a shot of espresso, basically a latte: *un café crème*
> A small milky coffee with a shot of espresso: *un petit café crème*
> Soy milk (typically available in speciality coffee shops only): *lait de soja*
> Decaf: *décafeiné*

Can you just fire some restaurant suggestions at me?
Sure thing. See 'Feeding a Broken Heart (or a Hangover)' on pg. 92, 'Eat like a Local' on pg. 127 or check 'Dining with the Cool Kids' on pg. 109. For some more tailored suggestions, try 'Date Night' on pg. 55 and 'Introducing your French Squeeze' on pg. 151. Eating on a tight budget? Find plenty of choice on pg. 23.

Where do locals actually go for some retail therapy?
'Shopping like a Parisian' on pg. 106.

Help! I'm coming to Paris with the love of my life and I'm proposing ...
Okay, we've got to get this right. Head over to 'Crazy in Love' on pg. 59 and 'Perfect for Popping the Question' on pg. 61.

I'm in Paris for a night and my flight gets in really late. Where can get a good bite to eat at any hour?
For something classic, Chez Denise. See 'While Paris is Sleeping', pg. 196, or cure your jet lag with a fix of Caribbean soul food at Babylone Bis on pg. 95. Both open all night.

Where should I take the kids?
Check out 'The Kids are Coming too' on pg. 152.

Where should we go for a night on the town?
I've got you covered in 'Nightcall' on pg. 114 and also check 'All Dressed Up & Nowhere to Go?' on pg. 97. If you're looking for a good dive bar, see pg. 17.

I'm planning a birthday surprise for my best friend. Got any suggestions?
For something playful during the daytime, you could celebrate with a picnic on your own little canal boat (pg. 154). Come happy hour, privatise an abandoned métro station (pg. 167).

I'm thinking of renting a car and getting out of town for the day, but I don't want to drive too far.
I've got a section for that called 'Get out of Town' (pg. 138).

Where can I take French-language course?
La Sorbonne (*Ccfs-sorbonne.fr*) or Institut Catholique de Paris (*En.icp.fr*).

I have to meet a client in Paris. Where should I suggest we meet?
For a creative coffee meeting, make it at Nuage Café (pg. 21), brainstorming over lunch or dinner, book a table at the Hôtel du Nord (*102 Quai de Jemmapes, 10ème; +33 1 40 40 78 78; open all day*). For client schmoozing, Septime (trendy option) on pg. 111 or Le Bon George (classic) on pg. 92.

What's the start-up scene like in Paris?
Paris is not Silicon Valley, but it doesn't want to be either. **The Family** is helping educate new entrepreneurs on how to crack the European start-up market with free workshops and meet-ups open to the public every week, hosted at their groovy headquarters in the Marais. (*thefamily.co/events*)

What's the deal with working in France as a foreigner?
Take a look at *Etudiantdeparis.fr/node/18*. Also see my list of places usually hiring ex-pats and handy tips for working in Paris on pg. 26.

Hôtel des Grandes Écoles

Where to Stay

Cheap & Cheerful

- **Hotel Dorado**: Bohemian chic digs at student rates, great for meeting other young travellers passing through. They also have a secret garden oasis at the back that comes in very handy during summer.
  (*17ème; eldoradohotel.fr*)
- **Hôtel des Grandes Ecoles**: Feel like you are miles away from a city, in the midst of the countryside, at this romantic and cosy hotel on the doorsteps of Ernest Hemingway's old apartment in Paris, minutes from the Latin Quarter, the Jardins Luxembourg and the Panthéon.
  (*5ème; hotel-grandes-ecoles.com*)
- **Le Mama Shelter**: Kitted out with Apple TVs, this edgy, contemporary and extremely comfortable hotel offers seriously bargain rates, and is located in an off-beat neighbourhood near Jim Morrison's grave.
  (*20ème; mamashelter.com/paris*)

Cosy & Quirky

- **Caron de Beaumarchais**: Perfect for time-travelling Marie Antoinettes. Upon entering, expect to feel like you might have interrupted Beaumarchais as he is finishing his final act of *The Marriage of Figaro*. A rare pianoforte, a card table that appears to have been abandoned midplay, candles and chandeliers recreate the atmosphere of an eighteenth-century private townhouse.
  (*3ème; carondebeaumarchais.com*)
- **Hôtel du Petit Moulin**: The hotel is built on the site of a boulangerie dating back to 1900 and before that, a seventeenth-century mill. The façade and sign of the boulangerie have been preserved, which is extremely picturesque. Christian Lacroix designed the hotel, which he describes as a dollhouse of 'seventeen ambiences that correspond to the seventeen ways of enjoying the Marais'.
  (*3ème; hotelpetitmoulinparis.com*)
- **Hôtel Henriette**: Ideal for a girly or romantic weekend, located in a little-known local 'village' tucked away in the 13th arrondissement, with tiny cobblestone streets and cute authentic bistros. Open your bedroom windows to a nice breeze and birds singing. A lovely place to unwind after a busy day in the city.
  (*13ème; hotelhenriette.com*)
- **Hôtel d'Angleterre**: Hemingway and his first wife Hadley stayed in room 14 for their first night in Paris, in December 1921. It was then the Hôtel Jacob, and before that the British Embassy, hence the current name. Pioneering aviator Charles Lindbergh also stayed here after completing the world's first non-stop solo flight from New York to Paris. Ask for a room on the ground floor surrounding the courtyard, where you'll have your own idyllic al fresco patio area for breakfast and apéro. It feels like you're living in your own Parisian cottage.
  (*6ème; hotel-dangleterre.com*)

Hip & Happening

Hôtel Providence Paris: Feel like you're living in an eccentric Parisian townhouse, surrounded by velvet everything, hosted by a worldly bohemian who enjoys late nights discussing anything taboo with a perfect Manhattan by the fire (pg. 109).
(*10ème; hotelprovidenceparis.com*)

Grand Amour Hôtel: Where the rock-star bands stay on tour. Each room is different, decorated with penis-themed carpeting, odd vintage accents found at auction, and anything that might make you feel like you've fallen down the rabbit hole and landed in a luxurious red-light-district pleasure house.
(*10ème; hotelamourparis.fr*)

Hôtel du Temps: A boutique hotel decorated in stylish vintage kitsch, you'll want to move in – or at least take the curtains home with you. The beautiful ground-floor bar is a good spot to hang with the local cool kids from 6pm.
(*9ème; hotel-du-temps.fr*)

Splurge on Something Special

Hôtel Particulier de Montmartre: Honeymooners in Paris can check into a luxurious villa nestled among trees in Montmartre that used to belong to the Hermès family. The hotel is also host to a very exclusive cocktail bar. It's such a gorgeous, one-of-a-kind place to stay in Paris, most guests can overlook the late-night weekend buzz.
(*18ème; hotel-particulier-montmartre.com*)

L'Hôtel: A mythical hotel where Oscar Wilde lived until his death. Princess Grace Kelly, Frank Sinatra and Elizabeth Taylor were also regulars. This is intimate luxury beyond the Four Seasons and far less boring. There's also a private underground cave pool to rent out all for yourself.
(*6ème; l-hotel.com*)

Saint James Paris: Stay in a grand nineteenth-century chateau near the Arc de Triomphe, surrounded by beautiful private gardens that were once the site of Paris's first air-balloon field in 1892. In an ode to its past, the terrace is decorated with tents shaped like hot air balloons and the splendid rooms (more like suites) have an *Alice in Wonderland* air about them. There are also two pavilions – three-storey stand-alone houses – that you can call home during your stay in Paris.
(*16ème; saint-james-paris.com*)

AirBnB more your thing?

I keep a wish list on the Airbnb website with my favourite hand-picked apartments, all located in hidden passageways or in the heart of the best neighbourhoods. I wouldn't recommend them otherwise. You can find my list, which I update regularly, here: *Airbnb.com/wishlists/112104048*.

PARIS

The 'What's Near Me?' Index

Feeling unsure of where to go next? Here, you'll find I've organised every address in this book by arrondissement (district) and ambience, to help you make the most out of every neighbourhood – or just to give you a little nudge in the right direction when you need it. Remember, the Parisian arrondissements are laid out like a clockwise snail's shell starting from the centre of the city, and one arrondissement is usually a walkable distance to the next. Paris is one of the most walkable cities in the world, after all...

KEY

French cuisine	Photo opportunity
International cuisine	People-watching
Have a glass of wine	Unusual/Underground
Cocktails	Coffee/Breakfast
Outdoor seating	Wellness
Museum	Hotel
Historic/Nostalgic	Workspace
For booklovers	Inspiring space
Kid friendly	Live entertainment
Dancing	Date spot
An excuse to dress up	Free or very light on the budget
Shopping	Spoil yourself
Related to the arts	Hidden/Hiding a special secret

1er Arrondissement

Dining

91 Au Bistro

56 Caveau du Palais

196 Chez Denise

110 Cibus

110 Davé

93 Ellsworth

131 Les Fines Gueules

155 Ma Salle à Manger

56 Verjus

Café Life & Night Life

39 Hemingway Bar at the Ritz Hotel

52 La Coquille

90 Le Bar de l'Entracte

183 Les Chandelles

97 The Beef Club Ballroom

55 Verjus Bar à Vins

Seeing & Doing

136 A L'Oriental

54 Didier Ludot

71 La Galcante

54 La Petite Robe Noir

63 Olympia Le Tan

52 Palais Royale

169 59 Rivoli

2ème Arrondissement

Dining

157 A Noste

95 Babylone Bis

95 Blend

113 Hero

95 Le Camion Qui Fume

94 Le Distrait

151 Le Grand Colbert

93 Les Bols de Jean

25 Pizza Popolare

154 Victoria Station-Wagon Restaurant

3ème Arrondissement

Dining

Café Life & Night Life

Seeing & Doing

4ème Arrondissement

Dining

5ème Arrondissement

Dining

Café Life & Night Life

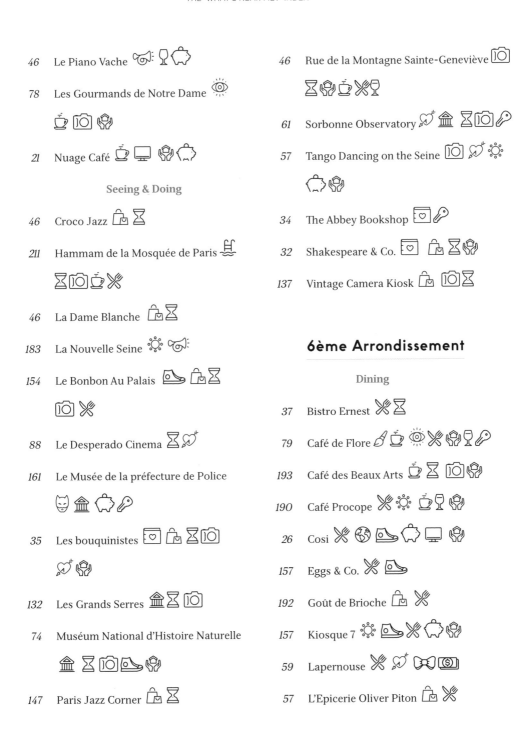

7ème Arrondissement

Dining

Seeing & Doing

8ème Arrondissement

Dining

Café Life & Night Life

Seeing & Doing

9ème Arrondissement

Dining

113 Hotel Amour 🍴🥤☀☕🛏👁

128 La Maison De La Culture Arménienne

🍴🌐⏳🐷🏷🗝

56 La Pétrelle 🍴⏳🖌💵🤲📷

92 Le Bon George 🍴⏳

92 Rue des Martyrs 🛍🍴☀☕👟

Café Life & Night Life

26 KB Café Shop ☕👟🍴🖥

118 L'Orphée 🥤🎧🗝

116 La Mano 🎧🥤👁

116 Le Carmen 🥤👁🎧🎀

116 Le Dépanneur Lounge 🥤☀👁

116 Le Mansart ☀🥤👁

114 Le Pigalle 🍴☕🥤👁🛏

116 Lulu White 🥤

97 Maison Souquet 🥤☕🛏⏳🎀 🪐💵

Seeing & Doing

134 Cité de Trévise 📷🗝

65 Cité Napoleon 📷🗝

78 Hôtel Drouot 🛍⏳🖌

61 Musée de la Vie Romantique 🏛🖌 🪐☀☕🤲

154 Musée Grevin 🏛⏳👟

76 Musée Gustave Moreau 🏛🖌 ⏳📷

47 Passage Jouffroy 🛍⏳📷

73 Phono Museum 🏛⏳👟📷 🐷🗝

74 Phonogalerie 🛍⏳🖌🗝

31 Rrose Sélavy Ateliers D'arts 🖌👟

134 Square Édouard VII 📷⏳🗝☕ 🤲

135 Théâtre Edouard VII 🎷📷⏳🗝

10ème Arrondissement

Dining

157   Bol Porridge Bar

56   Floyd's

109   Hôtel Providence

28   La Chambre Aux Oiseaux

93   Liberté

96   Nanashi

111   Ober Mama

59   Pink Flamingo

95   The Sunken Chip

25   Tribal Café

Café Life & Night Life

210   Centre Culturel Pouya

114   Gravity Bar

225   Grand Amour Hotel

117   La Java

89   Le Cinquante

20   Le Comptoir Générale

169   Point Éphémère

64   Rue Legouvé

64   Rue Sainte-Marthe

Seeing & Doing

20   Canal Saint-Martin

11ème Arrondissement

Dining

95   Au Ciel

127   Au Coin de Malte

109   Aux Deux Amis

93   Broken Biscuits

37   Café de l'Industrie

92   Chez Aline

131   Chez Paul

111   Clamato

12ème Arrondissement

Dining

151 L'Ebauchoir ✕ ☀ 🐷 ⬠

67 Marché Beauvau ✕ 🌐 ☀ 🛍 🐷

145 Le China Club ✕ 🌐 ⧗ 📢 🥤

Café Life & Night Life

117 Café de la Presse 💿 🥤 🐷 ⬠

Seeing & Doing

98 Barrio Latino 💿 🥤

104 Ground Control ☀ ✕ 🌐 👁 🐱 ☕ 🥤 💿 📷 👟

133 La Promenade Plantée ☀ 📷 ⧗ 🐷 🔑 🤲

152 Musée des Arts Forains 🏛 📷 ⧗ 👟 ☀ 🔑 🤲

64 Rue Crémieux 📷 🔑

60 Temple of Love 💘 📷 ☀ ⧗ 🐷 🔑

13ème Arrondissement

Dining

23 Chez Gladines ✕ 👟 🐷

167 La Maison des Frigos 🐱 🖌 ⧗ 📷 🐷 🔑

168 The Office Supper Club ✕ 🐱 🔑

Café Life & Night Life

105 OFF Paris Seine ☀ ✕ ☕ 🥤 🛏 🤲

Seeing & Doing

126 City of Flowers ⧗ 📷 ☀ 🔑

14ème Arrondissement

Dining

18 Jim Haynes's Parisian dinner parties ✕ ☀ 📷 🐷 🔑

Seeing & Doing

123 Country Bumpkin Lane 📷 ⧗ 🔑

239

15ème Arrondissement

Seeing & Doing

16ème Arrondissement

Dining

Seeing & Doing

17ème Arrondissement

Dining

18ème Arrondissement

Dining

Café Life & Night Life

Seeing & Doing

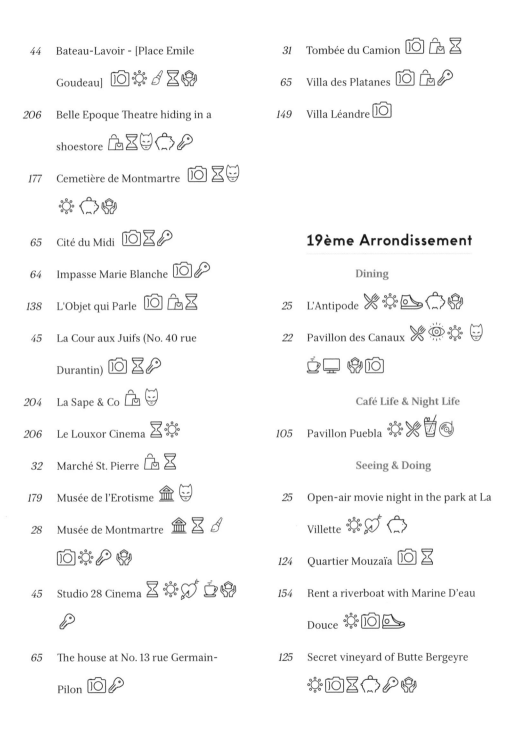
19ème Arrondissement

Dining

Café Life & Night Life

Seeing & Doing

20ème Arrondissement

Dining

214 Café Au Folies ✂️🥤👁️🐷

111 Dilia ✂️👁️💵

109 Grand Bain 🍴🍷👁️

146 La Bellevilloise 🍴☀️🥤📣🐱 📷👟

23 La Cantine de Belleville ✂️🐷

95 Mama Shelter 🍴🌍 ☀️🍷🥤 👟🛏️🛒🖥️

Café Life & Night Life

124 Café Lumière ✂️🍷☀️☕🤲

124 Eva Pritsky ✂️🍷🛍️⏳ 🐱🐷🔑

217 La Fontaine Henri IV 🍷☀️⏳📷 🪴🐷

Seeing & Doing

32 La Maroquinerie ✂️📣🍷☀️🐷

165 La Petite Ceinture ⏰🐱📷

133 Le Jardin des Soupirs ☀️📷🐷🔑

97 Salsa dancing at Studio de l'Ermitage 🥤🎧

124 The 'Other' Montmartre 📷🔑⏳

178 The X-Rated Paris Grave ⏳🐱🐷📷☀️

64 Villa de l'Ermitage 📷🔑⏳

Shopping

214 Bazar de Belleville 🛍️🐱🐷

Near or just outside Paris

Dining

49 Chez Louisette ✂️📣⏳🔑

157 Ma Cocotte ✂️☀️👟☕

Café Life & Night Life

158 Trianon Palace Hotel 🍴☕🥤💵 ☀️🛏️🎀

Seeing & Doing

138 Barbizon 🏛️🖌️✂️⏳📷☀️🤲

173 Chateau Rothschild ⏳📷🐱

31 Daniel et Lili 🛍️⏳🖌️🐷

Merci!

Thank you, Alex, for letting me fall in love with Paris (and you) on the back of your scooter.

Thank you Mum for being my unwavering fan throughout all my questionable escapades, and to my selfless Pa for your quiet understanding. Thank you both for insisting I give Paris a go, and for always wanting the best for me, even when I didn't.

Thank you to my friends who lent a hand in exchange for glasses of wine. Nayeli, for first sitting down with me in that café by the canal where we scribbled down a plan for this book together on a wine-stained napkin. McCallum, for your mutual love of this city and that finger of yours, always on the pulse.

Thank you to Julia Celms, the loveliest and most eager intern who assisted with the fact-checking and photography of this book, venturing to all corners of the city clutching my 'Still To-Do' list.

Thank you to my publisher, Roads, for believing that this messy blogger could actually write a book – and for all those extended deadlines.

And finally, thank you to readers of *Messy Nessy Chic*; my little community of internetters who became my friends, my supporters and now my muse too.

Rambling Notes of a Traveller

_____

_____

_____

_____

_____

_____

_____

_____

_____

_____

_____

_____

_____

_____

_____

_____

_____

_____

_____